# Whole Lotta Shakin' Goin' On

Robert Cain

# Whole Lotta Shakin' Goin' On

## Jerry Lee Lewis

The Dial Press 🦁 New York

Published by
The Dial Press
1 Dag Hammarskjold Plaza
New York, New York 10017

Manufactured in the United States of America

First printing

Design by James L. McGuire

Library of Congress Cataloging in Publication Data

Cain, Robert J
   Whole Lotta Shakin' Goin' On.

   Discography: p.
   1. Lewis, Jerry Lee.   2. Singers—United States—Biography.   3. Rock musicians—United States—Biography.   4. Country musicians—United States—Biography.   I. Title.
ML420.L        784.5'4'00924    [B]        80-27188
   ISBN 0-8037-4490-0

To Blanche Cain,
and all of those
who love rock 'n' roll,
for they shall be
forever young

# Acknowledgments

It has been said that "Success has many parents, failure is an orphan." If this be true, then the successful completion of this project must be shared with all of the warm and gracious people who supplied valuable data, photos, and anecdotes and granted interviews.

Steve Allen, Mickey Gilley, Tommy Thomas, Tom Jones, Shelby Singleton (and Doris Kelley), Jerry Kennedy (and Trish Williams), Harvey Palash (of Diamond P Productions, Los Angeles), Sammy Jackson (of radio station KLAC, Los Angeles), Gary Skala, Kay Martin, Mike Kasebo, Jim Patino, Bill Justis, Alan Clark, Ann Konigsberg (in the Publicity Department of Electra Records, Los Angeles), and finally the Publicity Department of Mercury/Phonogram Records in Chicago.

Special thanks to Frankie Jean Lewis (Mrs. Marion Terrell) and to Ken Griffis (advisor to the John Edwards Memorial Foundation) for granting permission to reproduce portions of the documentary "This Is Jerry Lee."

**PHOTO CREDITS:** Title page, George Rodriguez, *Country Fever* magazine; pages 1, 3, 4, 5, 6, Frankie Jean Lewis; 7, Rhett Powell; 9, UPI; 11, 12, Alan Clark; 15, Steve Allen; 16, Frankie Jean Lewis; 17, 19, UPI; 20, Michael Ochs Archives; 21, Gary Skala; 23, Michael Ochs Archives; 25, 26, Wide World Photos; 27, 28, 32, 33, UPI; 35, 39, Mickey Gilley; 43, Alan Clark; 44, UPI; 54, Shelby Singleton; 59, Alan Clark; 61, 63, 65, 66, Steve Allen; 83, Jim Jeffries; 86, 87, 88, 89, 90, 91, 92, 93, Jasper Dailey; 95, 97, 99, Ahmanson Theatre, Los Angeles; 103, Wide World Photos; 109, Tom Jones; 113, Rita Gillespie; 115, 117, Mercury Records; 120, Jasper Dailey; 127, James R. Reid.

# Contents

# Whole Lotta Shakin' Goin' On

With his father, Elmo, and mother, Mary Ethel.

# 1
# The Early Years

I came out jumping and I've been
running ever since.

Jerry Lee Lewis

September 29, 1935, at Turtle Lake on the Calhoun plantation, just a few miles from Ferriday, Louisiana, a child was born to Mary and Elmo Lewis. This boy would grow up to shape musical history and become a legend in his own time. He would be called The Killer. He was christened Jerry Lee Lewis.

Jerry was the second of four children born to Elmo and Mary Ethel Lewis, and together they made a closely knit, loving, deeply religious family. Young Jerry Lee was raised just as thousands of other Bible Belt youngsters before him, with great emphasis on love of family and the importance of strong religious convictions.

When Jerry was only three, his nine-year-old brother, Elmo, Jr., was killed in a tragic automobile accident. When the intoxicated driver was apprehended by the local police, he was told there would be no charges brought against him, for they had been told to let him go. "Just let the good Lord take care of this—we'll put it in God's hands" was the comment made by Mother Lewis.

The Lewis family was a musical one, so it was not surprising that young Jerry began his career at the age of eight. While most boys his age were playing cowboys and Indians or wondering why girls were built differently, Jerry was already practicing on his father's six-string guitar. He would often bring the guitar to school to entertain the other students with his picking and singing. His music came naturally, and he reveled in his classmates' attention. He dreamed heady dreams. The seed had been planted.

Jerry recalls the first time he sang solo before an audience.

*I was brought up in the Assembly of God church in Ferriday, Louisiana . . . Holiness Church. I used to play the piano for the choir and sing. Of course, we had no special choir—anybody could come up and sing—and this is really where I sang my first song, and I was eight—not nine—eight. I walked up and started singing. So, of course, I forgot the words to it—I couldn't even think of nothing. There was folks sitting out there, about forty people out there. I was really somethin'. I really got shook up and, very politely, I walked over to my mother and I said, "Momma, what was that song I was supposed to sing?" and she said, "What Will My Answer Be," and so I went back up and I sang it, and ever since then I've been singing.*

The guitar captured his interest for quite a while—until he discovered the piano. As the story goes, nine-year-old Jerry noticed a piano at his Aunt Stella's home, climbed up on the stool, and began to plunk out a tune on it, much to everyone's amazement. His father, Elmo, was so impressed with his ability to play at such a young age that he mortgaged their modest home to buy him a piano: a used Stark upright.

For Jerry Lee, it was love at first sight. At first he practiced one, then two, then three hours a day, eventually even longer. "He was *obsessed* with it." His sister Frankie Jean remembers vividly:

*Jerry would play his piano sometimes eleven or twelve hours a day and then he would pause and have food brought to him*

The house in which Jerry Lee was born at Turtle Lake, Louisiana.

and then he would just continue to play. Of course, it paid off real well. Mother encouraged him constantly.

Frankie Jean Lewis remembers:

*He was the favorite. He just had more charm and more personality. Jerry and Elvis: I guess they were alike in many ways, especially the family ties. I met Elvis right before his first record came out. He was extremely close to his mother—extremely close. Jerry and his mother were even closer. I don't know, they just had something . . . togetherness. They were just inseparable. After Elmo Jr.'s death, I guess she turned everything, her thoughts and everything, toward Jerry Lee. Mother and Daddy could not get over Jerry's talent.*

When asked about the rest of her talented family, Frankie Jean replies:

*We all sang in church. I played very little. Linda plays real well, but I just couldn't. I took piano lessons, but it just didn't work out. Of course, Jerry took the lead. There just wasn't any way we could compete with his piano playing. Daddy encouraged him also. They wouldn't let him work in the field or do anything like that. They wouldn't want anything to happen to his hands. Jerry wasn't allowed to drive the tractor or things like that.*

As a young boy Jerry Lee was quick, alert, and energetic. However, it soon became obvious that the life of a scholar was not for him. Papa Lewis recalled those early days:

*He was a good boy, but he didn't go to school too much. We sent him to school and I found out he was in the swimming pool—oh, about one half of the time. He came in on the last day and brought in his* report, and it would be right up to date, and we was tickled to death, his mother and I. We just thought he was doing great. Come to find out he was over in the swimming pool.

Young Jerry pursued his musical obsession with youthful exuberance. He listened to the radio, listened to the neighborhood jukebox, then tried to recall and play those songs—and amazingly he did. Jerry's ability to remember lyrics and melodies was astounding.

Two cousins shared his passion for music: Mickey Gilley and Jimmy Swaggart. Today Jimmy Swaggart is a very famous minister with the Assemblies of God church in Mississippi. Reverend Swaggart reminisces about growing up in Ferriday:

In 1950.

Jerry Lee's mother was my mother's sister, and his dad was my dad's uncle, so that makes us first cousins and a half, if you can feature such a thing. Jerry Lee and I were raised together almost like brothers. We were always in the same house continually, and we were together incessantly— I suppose for the first ten years of our lives. About the first memories I have of me and Jerry [are of] playing in church together and playing piano together—starting back when we were just children. Jerry was tremendously talented. As far as singing as a child, he was just fantastic. Maybe I am a little biased or prejudiced, but I never heard anybody that I felt could compare with him singing. He was just literally fantastic with natural talent. Even today I don't think anybody in the world for rhythm music can outplay Jerry Lee.

For many years Jerry has proclaimed himself to be a completely self-taught musician. This is basically true; however, Reverend Swaggart comments:

He took maybe one or two lessons. I took about the same number from the same teacher. The teacher started us out with some little one, two, three stuff. I forgot exactly what it was. We could already play, but Jerry Lee was very proficient, and he would tell Jerry Lee to play some little old ditty from some little old book, and Jerry would start playing one of the top tunes of that particular day. He was excellent, even then. That would make the teacher mad. I remember Jerry Lee said something to him one time, and the man slapped him. I don't know what developed after that. Of course, when Jerry Lee became popular, they became very fast and very close friends.

Young Jerry and his cousin Jimmy Swaggart often sneaked into Haney's Big House, a local dance hall, to watch the performers onstage. With wide-eyed fascination, the two youngsters listened while the black combos and big bands blared their soulful sounds.

When asked to remember who played there, Lewis replied:

*B.B. King, Ray Charles, Duke Ellington—all the cats, man. They came in big buses, you know. Great, great people. I used to sneak in that place, man, and Haney run it. Great big Negro man, fine person . . . knew him all my life . . . great people. I used to slip in, hide in there. Me and Jimmy Swaggart, we would hear these cats playing and—B.B. King, like, was a real young kid himself. Haney would catch us and run us out. He would say, "Man, your uncle Lee catch you in here." My uncle Lee Calhoun, you know—he was something else. He owned half the city. "He catch you in here, he'd kill us all." But those were great days, back when I was eight, nine years old.*

This early exposure at Haney's to the rhythm and blues of B.B King and Ray Charles undoubtedly had its influence on young Jerry's style of piano. However, when asked if the artists at Haney's affected him, he replied:

*No, not really. I never had an influence on my piano style. I taught myself on the piano everything I know. Of course, naturally, I had a God-given talent—I really did. What you are talking about is whether I was blessed with gathering this talent through other artists. I've often thought about this: I don't know.*

It was during these formative years that the distinctive Lewis boogie-woogie style began to jell, producing a strange blend of country music laced with a heavy beat. A decade later this fusion of black and white rhythms, plus a dash of frenzy, would be dubbed rockabilly, later called rock 'n' roll.

Jerry continued to play and sing at the nearby Assembly of God church along with his cousin, Jimmy Swaggart, and the church became an important showcase for young Jerry's blossoming talents.

At about the age of twelve, Jerry Lee heard a record by Al Jolson, a legendary entertainer of another era. The song was "Down Among the Sheltering Pines," and young Jerry was highly impressed. Immediately he ran home and sang it and has been a Jolson fan ever since. When asked to name the four greatest song stylists of all time, he remarks:

*Al Jolson is Number One. Jimmie Rodgers, the Singing Brakeman, is Number Two. Number Three is Hank Williams, the Hillbilly Shakespeare. And Number Four—of course—is Jerry Lee Lewis.*

Jerry was just thirteen years old when he played his first nightclub engagement. It was at the Blue Cat Club in Natchez, Mississippi, and he earned ten dollars a night. (During the day he was going to school.) Later he played the Hilltop Club, then the Wagon Wheel, where he worked with a trio for six dollars a night. The Blue Cat Club in Natchez was a long way from Las Vegas or Broadway, but a star that was to be had already begun to shine.

Jerry Lee's father was a farmer and carpenter, a muscular man who stood six foot four and weighed close to two hundred pounds. Elmo Lewis's great strength was a valuable asset, for his work as a carpenter took him and his family to many little towns

With school chum David Beatty, now the Reverend Beatty of Baton Rouge.

in Louisiana. Times were tough and jobs hard to get: in order to find work, he had to move with his family frequently. In one year alone, they moved thirteen times! Where the Lewis family went, so did their piano, and Elmo was the official piano mover.

Papa Lewis's skill as a piano mover also helped the Lewis family earn money during lean periods. He would lift the old Stark upright onto the back of his battered truck, he and young Jerry Lee would head for town and unload the piano, Jerry would put on a show, and Elmo would pass the hat. Back on the truck went the piano, and on the way home they'd count their money.

Jerry made his first real public appearance in a car lot in Ferriday when he was about fourteen. The local Ford agency was promoting its new cars, and the entertainment was supplied by a small country and western group. Jerry performed a number of songs including "Drinking Wine Spo-dee-o-dee." The crowd was pleased. After passing the hat, Jerry collected the enormous sum of ten dollars! It was the first time young Jerry had heard what he sounded like over a PA system.

As a young boy, he had several very close friends. One was Mickey Gilley, another was Jimmy Swaggart, and a third was Cecil Harrelson. In later years Cecil would become Jerry's road manager and brother-in-law. At the age of sixteen Jerry and Cecil decided to try their luck and head for the big city. Cecil recalled their first trip to New Orleans:

*We decided we would leave home and go make a living for ourselves, so we went and got a bus in Ferriday, La. We got a bus that went to New Orleans. We went down there and we tried to get everyone to listen to us. We made every joint in New Orleans. We didn't know anything. We were just kids, and everybody said, "Man, you're good, you're good." "You're good," but that was it. So we went to a little record studio down there. I think it was B & J or*

WELCOME TO . . . . .
FERRIDAY
FERRIDAY WOMAN'S CLUB 50 Yrs. 1929 - 1979
MICKEY GILLEY HOWARD K. SMITH
HOME OF
JERRY LEE LEWIS JIMMY SWAGGART

*maybe it was J & B Record Studio, and we paid for it ourselves. Jerry cut a demo record. Just him and the piano. First time he ever recorded anything on wax.*

Cecil continued:

*Jerry was always a little taller than I. I would only stand five feet eight inches, but Jerry, when he was growing up, he was just a skinny boy, you know, and he was very strong for his age, but he was always a musician. He had very tremendous strength for his age. I know because we used to get into a lot of scrapes that would prove it. His main goal in life ever since I have ever known him has been music, and he would sit on the piano everywhere that we went; in fact, he and I, we would go into these bars or something, you know, and I would con the man running the bar to let him play the piano or something, and he would go up, and naturally when Jerry*

*sat at the piano, they wanted to hire him, and we used to do this all the time.*

Upon leaving high school, Jerry enrolled in the Bible Institute of Waxahatchie (in Waxahatchie, Texas), and his mother had hopes he would become a gospel preacher. This dream was short-lived. At a student gathering Jerry's natural tendency to play everything with a boogie-woogie beat got the best of him. The faculty did not appreciate his rocking version of "My God Is Real," and he was suspended for two weeks. He never returned.

What followed was a succession of odd jobs. He tried working in the oil fields: that lasted about three days—it was too hard. The job he remembers most clearly was selling sewing machines door to door.

*People would fill out cards and things, these little cards in the grocery stores, and they would give away a sewing machine. Actu-*

ally, it was just a phony bunch of junk, which I didn't know or I would never have gotten into it. People would buy the groceries, fill out the card, and turn it in, and they did give away a sewing machine, but they would take all the other cards and give them to us peons, so to speak, and I would go up to the people's door, knock on the door, and say, "Good evening, lady, this is Jerry Lee Lewis. I'm from the ____ Sewing Center from back in Baton Rouge, Louisiana. I would like to say you are the happy winner of a ____ sewing machine, I mean fifty dollars off." I was a great salesman. I was only eighteen years old. Just a poor kid trying to struggle along, make a living, and I was selling the hell out of sewing machines. I guarantee you one thing: I sold more sewing machines than Carter['s] got liver pills. Matter of fact, I sold so many one time, I like to got locked up. Played a good trick on them. I won't get into that because the district attorney down there still don't know the true story.

None of these odd jobs lasted very long because Jerry had been bitten by the show business bug. In 1956 he decided to head for Memphis to audition for Sam Phillips, who had already made rockabilly stars of Elvis Presley and Carl Perkins.

# "Whole Lotta Shakin'"

> Just point me to the piano and give
> me my money. In fifteen minutes I'll
> have 'em shaking, shouting, shivering,
> and shacking.
>
> Jerry Lee Lewis

**T**he year is 1956. "Ike" Eisenhower sits in the White House for a second term, Yul Brynner wins an Oscar for his stunning performance in *The King and I,* Floyd Patterson captures the heavyweight boxing championship, the New York Yankees defeat the Brooklyn Dodgers to win the World Series, and America is in the midst of a musical revolution, a youthful rebellion. It's called rock 'n' roll.

For the first time in history the teenagers of America are speaking in one collective voice and demanding an identity all their own. When social historians write the story of the fifties, it must include the emergence of teenage fashions, of a distinctive teenage language, of exclusively teenage dance crazes, and most of all of a teenage music which created a whole new life-style.

Fading fast from the radio were such long-time favorites as Vic Damone, Eddie Fisher, Rosemary Clooney, Doris Day, and Perry Como. New songs and even newer performers were exploding over the airwaves. By the summer of 1956 such teenage idols as Elvis Presley, Fats Domino, Little Richard, Ivory Joe Hunter, Clyde McPhatter, Frankie Lymon and the Teenagers, Chuck Berry, the Platters, and Roy Hamilton were dominating the air waves, much to the alarm of the adult population of America. It mattered little to the kids that most of these performers were black; what mattered most was the beat. Songs with a beat were sweeping across the country like an epidemic.

Parents were not the only ones who were shocked by this new rock 'n' roll fad: most of the major record companies found it just as baffling. Columbia, Mercury, Capitol, and Decca were caught with their musical pants down. All of these giants had millions of dollars invested in huge rosters of established artists like Bing Crosby, Frankie Laine, Perry Como, Tony Martin, Tony Bennett, Patti Page, Frank Sinatra, Johnnie Ray, Doris Day, etc., whose record sales had begun to slump at an alarming rate. Another peculiar phenomenon of rock 'n' roll music of the fifties was the fact that it seemed to be the exclusive domain of small independent record labels. Such tiny labels as Chess, Checker, Specialty, Federal, Dootone, Vee Jay, Duke, Paradise, Savoy, Modern, and Atlantic seemed to have little trouble getting one hit after another into the top forty, while the majors were still trying to figure out what the hell was going on.

Without a doubt, the foremost example of a small independent label to achieve astounding success was Sun Records. Most music historians would agree that the major catalyst of this new musical revolution was Sun Records and their incredible collection of rockabilly stars, which included Carl Perkins, Jerry Lee Lewis, Roy Orbison, Charlie Rich, and Johnny Cash. Clearly, the brightest of these stars was Jerry Lee Lewis.

Of all the talents spawned by Sam Phillips on Sun, Jerry Lee Lewis and his pumping piano was the wildest. This platinum blond, piano-pounding pied piper of rock 'n' roll added a new dimension to playing the piano. He kicked it. He leaped on top of it. He pulverized it. He sent the piano stool flying across the stage!

Most rock entertainers were satisfied with mere applause: not so with Jerry Lee. His frantic antics were designed to bring a

about it, and we collected—well, I should say, gathered all the eggs, for about three weeks. We had thirty-three dozen and sold the eggs, and we took the money and we went to Memphis, and I auditioned for Jack Clement, who worked for Sam Phillips at the time, and this is where I got my start. He cut some tapes on me because I insisted on it. I said, "If you don't do it, I am going out to Sam Phillips's house," and he said, "Well, he's in Miami, Florida, on vacation." I said, "I don't care where he's at. I'll park on his doorstep for three weeks until he hears me" . . . and he heard me. I didn't park on his doorstep, but anyway he [Jack Clement] played the tapes for him. I came back about a month later and as I walked in the door, I met Jack Clement walking out, and he said, "Well, Jerry Lewis"—he didn't call me Jerry Lee Lewis—"I was just fixin' to call you. Sam [Phillips] heard your tapes and he liked them and he wants to cut a session on you." So I cut "Crazy Arms." "Crazy Arms" stirred up a lot of noise, and we sold about 300,000 records on it.

"Crazy Arms" did surprisingly well on the country and western charts. Considering the fact that the song had been recorded earlier that same year by C & W giant Ray Price, it seems even more surprising. But then Jerry Lee was never one to shy away from competition. In later years, many of his biggest hits would come from rerecording songs which were originally introduced by other artists.

Bill Justis, who had a huge hit himself on Sun in the fifties with "Raunchy," was in the studio when Jerry Lee auditioned. He relates how Jerry Lee's audition turned into his first recording session:

*I was in there one day visiting with Jack Clement, who was the A & R [artist and repertoire] man there, and Jack introduced me to Jerry and also Jerry's uncle. The name struck me right away—because of*

crowd to its feet, clapping their hands, dancing wildly in the aisles and shouting to a frenzied state of delicious pandemonium.

How did it all begin? For young Jerry Lee it all started with a three-hundred-mile journey to Memphis and a display of stubbornness that would embarrass a Missouri mule. Although many years have passed since then, Jerry Lee still remembers it all very clearly.

*I read a magazine about Elvis Presley, and Sam Phillips and Jud Phillips helping Elvis Presley get started. I asked my daddy*

*the comedian Jerry Lewis. He [Jerry Lee] said, "Be sure don't forget that Lee, man"—you know the way he talks. Jack Clement proceeded to have Jerry and his uncle sit down and play, and make an audition tape for Sam Phillips. Jerry's uncle—I forget whether it was an electric bass or a guitar that he played, but I know that one of his hands was messed up because he had had an accident. They got the drummer and just started playing. Jerry did two or three things, I remember. You know, it was not a record session; it was an audition. Somebody maybe at the other end of the studio would open the door and walk through, and all that. Well, out of that, when Sam heard Jerry Lee do "Crazy Arms," he released it. It wasn't like any giant at that time: it was maybe territorial and it was very encouraging. It did sell quite a few records.*

If the sales of "Crazy Arms" were encouraging, then the sales for Jerry's next record must have been overwhelming to Sam Phillips and his tiny but talented crew at Sun. Jerry's second release from the Sun studios was another up-tempo number entitled "Whole Lotta Shakin' Goin' On," coupled with "It'll Be Me," which was written by his producer, Jack Clement. Reminiscing about the historic recording session which produced "Shakin'," Jerry said,

*I did "A Whole Lotta Shakin' " for him (Jack Clement), and he said, "Oh boy, now wait a minute. Elvis has done drove this into the ground and broke it off—it's all over! You gotta have something different." I told him, "I'm gonna tell you something, Jack, I'm a hit. Just cut me a record, boy."*

To say that "Whole Lotta Shakin' " was a hit is an understatement. It sold a million copies almost instantly. By the time it reached the two million mark it was Number One not only on the pop charts but on the rhythm and blues and country and western charts also. It remains to this day one of the few records in musical history to achieve such incredible popularity in all three areas at once. It has been estimated that the disk has sold well over twenty million copies (on Sun, Smash, Pickwick, etc.) worldwide.

Another surprising thing about "Shakin' " is the fact that it was recorded in one take, at the end of a recording session. Jack Clement just turned on the tape, Jerry Lee sat down at the piano, and two minutes and fifty-two seconds later one of the largest-selling records of all time had emerged.

One might assume that the record just jumped to the top of the charts with little or no difficulty, but this was not the case. Initially it was banned by numerous radio stations as being too suggestive for airplay. Considering the strict moral climate of that period (1957) one can easily imagine why.

Although not erotic by today's relaxed standards, it was scorned by parents in the late fifties who considered its lyric content shocking and disgusting.

"They said at the time, in 1957, that this was the most *risqué* record that they had ever heard." Jerry Lee recalled,

*BMI banned it, every radio station banned*
*it, every television station where it was*
*played on banned it. It was ridiculous—playing a record like that, I mean.*

It was Jerry's first run-in with public morality and the surprising influence that it could bring to bear on radio and television networks. His initial clash with the establishment was a minor one, but not his last.

What Jerry needed most at this point in his career was major television exposure, similar to that which Elvis had enjoyed by his appearances on the Steve Allen and Ed Sullivan shows. This much-needed network boost would come through the interest and diligence of Sam Phillips's brother Jud, who took Jerry to New York for his initial shot at the big time. Reflecting on his first visit to the Big Apple, Jerry said,

*Jud Phillips came to me in Florence, Alabama. We were doing a show there, and he came to me and he told me, "I like what you're doing—this song 'Whole Lotta Shakin' Goin' On.' I believe I can take you to New York City and I can get you a national television show, and we can sell some records on this thing, and you can really be a big hit off of it." I was twenty-one years old—a kid. I said to him, "My Lord, I'll do anything." Johnny Cash was there, and Carl Perkins. Johnny said, "Hey, why don't you take me?" Carl said the same thing. We were sitting around eating sardines, onions, and crackers—this is the truth—sitting over at Jud's house. Anyway, we went to New York City: I was reading comic books (Superman and everything), and Jud was working hard. We went to Steve Allen, walked in and auditioned for him. It's a great story.*

In the words of Jud Phillips, the man who made it all happen:

*When I saw the action in Jerry and saw it was not a gimmick like I'd fooled with with other artists—that it was real, real action—I went to him and told him I would like to take him to New York and talk to Ed Sullivan. That's the primary objective of going up there, and Ed turned us down—said he wouldn't be interested. So, I got a hold of Henry Frankel, who was talent coordinator for NBC, and I got him to get a hold of Jules Green, who was Steve Allen's man-ager, and see if he could get a little conference with him and talk to him about Jerry. Henry set it up and Jules said, "We'll give him fifteen minutes and see what he's got." So we went over to Jules's office, and he said, "Well, Jud, have you got any pictures of this man?" I said, "Nope." He said, "Well, has he had a record out?" I said, "Yes, he's got a record out now." He said, "How long has it been out?" I said, "Several months." "How many has it sold?" "About thirty thousand." He sez, "Well, Henry, here is a salesman without anything to sell." I said, "No, I brought my product with me." He said, "Well, that's better!" "He's leaning up against the wall over there." Jerry was just as unconcerned as he could be, you know. "Well, if you'll clean off that piano and let him sit down at the piano, I think you will see that this is an ac-tion artist all the way." Well, they cleaned the piano off, and Jerry went over and sat down and started playing, "A Whole Lotta Shakin'." At that time Jules wasn't con-cerned: he still had his feet up on his desk, not even looking around or showing any interest at all. When Jerry cut loose on "Whole Lotta Shakin'," he and Henry both got up, went around behind the piano, and stood there and watched him. Then Jules said, "I'll give you $500 right now if you take him back to the room and let nobody see him until nine o'clock in the morning, when Steve [Allen] gets in." So the next morning Steve came in, and we sat down and had the meeting. He really liked it, he dug it. He saw the action in it. But there were some in his organization who said, "No, we can't do this because this man hasn't had a record out, because he has never been on the charts." I told him, "All I'm asking you to do is give this man three minutes of TV exposure, and any audience that you have at the time he starts, you'll have them when he finishes. The next time around you will have a tremendous audi-ence!" So they decided finally to let us do* *this and then they took an option for two more shows.*

Jud had succeeded in getting Jerry booked for the show, but there was still another major obstacle to overcome. BMI (Broadcast Music, Inc.) had banned his song, which meant that even if Jerry appeared on the show, he could not perform "Whole Lotta Shakin'." Jud explains how he handled the dilemma.

*BMI had banned it because of one or two little words in it, which is ridiculous for them to do. But Steve had already given me the contract on the first show, and I called BMI and told them, "You ban this song and* *you're in trouble because we're going to play this song on* The Steve Allen Show," *and immediately they lifted the ban on the song.*

Jerry was immediately scheduled to perform on Sunday, July 28, 1957, and perform he did! He sang "Crazy Arms" and "Whole Lotta Shakin'" in his now typical wild and stormy fashion. The public's reaction to his performance was astounding. Overnight *The Steve Allen Show* had brought young Jerry Lee to the attention of millions of TV viewers across the U.S., and overnight he became a superstar.

When Jerry made his second appearance on Steve's show (on August 11, 1957), he

First appearance on *The Steve Allen Show*—July 28, 1957.

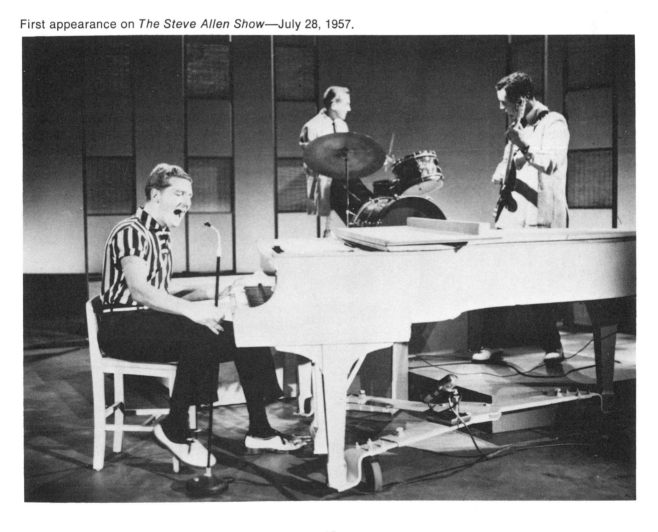

gave a performance of "Shakin' " that would have easily registered 8.9 on the Richter Scale. That memorable second show in August received such a high rating that it decisively beat the reigning Sunday night champ, Ed Sullivan, in the TV rating duel.

Steve Allen remembers his initial impressions of the young, skinny "wild man" from Ferriday.

*He was a kind of wild, swinging, boogie-woogie screamer when I came into contact with him when he was booked for our show. We had gotten some good reports of him doing some things in Nashville and places of that sort. As I recall, whenever you booked people who worked in that abandoned fashion, that physically free fashion, in those days, you used to get complaints. I think we all remember the public controversy over Elvis Presley. As a matter of fact, when we booked him [Elvis]—since ours was primarily a comedy show—we generally worked comedy values into the presentation of almost everything except the reading of the Lord's Prayer or something of that sort. So we were attracted by the fact that Jerry Lee was funny in addition to being good and keeping swinging time and all that. But in those days, as I said, you would get complaints.*

After his highly successful appearance on *The Steve Allen Show*, Jerry next appeared on Alan Freed's *Big Beat Party* TV show (on August 2, 1957). At that point Alan Freed was the undisputed king of rock 'n' roll disc jockeys. Next Jerry performed "Whole Lotta Shakin' " on a new TV dance show called *American Bandstand*, hosted by a boyish-looking Dick Clark. Dick Clark remembers it clearly:

*I think the first time Jerry Lee ever appeared he came to Philadelphia to appear on the* Bandstand *in late 1957. He probably did "Whole Lotta Shakin' Goin' On." Sub-*

*sequent to that, in February—February fourteenth, to be exact, of 1958—he appeared on* Dick Clark's Saturday Night [Beechnut] Show, *which was a rock 'n' roll extravaganza from the Little Theater off Times Square in New York City, and he performed "Whole Lotta Shakin' Goin' On" and "Great Balls of Fire." We had explosions going on in the background, and older people who looked at this thing must have thought we had gone insane!*

In 1957 Dick Clark and his *American Bandstand* show were just emerging as an influential force in the rock scene. In later years Dick Clark would dethrone Alan Freed as the king of rock 'n' roll DJs. *American Bandstand* would become the most important single TV production for the promotion and perpetuation of rock music.

November 3, 1957—Jerry makes his third guest appearance on *The Steve Allen Show* to introduce his latest single, which is aptly titled "Great Balls of Fire." Result: another

million seller—five million, to be exact. "Great Balls of Fire" is penned by the talented Otis Blackwell, who also wrote "All Shook Up" and "Don't Be Cruel" for Elvis and "Good Golly Miss Molly" for frantic Little Richard.

November 4, 1957—Jerry performs "Whole Lotta Shakin' " and "Great Balls of Fire" for his third appearance on *American Bandstand*. With all of this national promotion and publicity, is it any wonder that "Whole Lotta Shakin' " goes on to become a rock classic? In later years John Lennon of the Beatles will refer to it as the perfect rock 'n' roll record.

Later that year Jerry appeared as a guest star in his first major motion picture. He performed "Great Balls of Fire" in the Warner Brothers' movie *Jamboree*. He was featured along with many other prominent rock performers of that era, including Fats Domino, Buddy Know, Jimmy Bowen, Charlie Gracie, the Four Coins, and fellow Sun artist Carl Perkins. Warner Brothers Records pressed a small number (twenty-five to fifty) of the movie sound-track album for *Jamboree,* which were to be sent to disc jockeys all over the country. They were to be used as a promotional tool, which was a common practice of that period. When the artists involved saw the final printed album cover, almost all of them were displeased with their billing. Many of them (or their agents) complained loudly to Warner Bros. Records. Since there were eighteen different artists involved, including Connie Francis, Frankie Avalon, Slim Whitman, Jodie Sands, and Count Basie, the dilemma seemed insoluble. In a fit of frustration Warner Bros. canceled all future plans to commercially release the *Jamboree* disk, thereby making it instantly a collector's item. Today the record sells for $100 a copy, *if* you can find it.

Early in 1956 Jerry's price per show was $50. By the end of '57 his fee had catapulted to $10,000 a night. Not bad for a twenty-two-year-old kid from the backwoods of Louisiana with no formal musical training whatsoever. For young Jerry Lee Lewis the American dream of success had become real.

Linda Gail Lewis, Jerry's talented sister, was very young when "Shakin' " made Number One, but she remembers:

*Of course, I was very proud of Jerry: my whole family was, and it was thrilling for us because we had never had anything financially, and all of a sudden Jerry was a very wealthy young man and he always shared everything with his family, and we had everything we wanted—new cars, clothes, homes. My sister [Frankie Jean] went on a trip to Europe and, oh, it was great—it was like something you see in the movies. It doesn't happen usually to everyday people.*

Many music historians believe that the year 1956 *belonged* to Elvis Presley. The incredible impact Elvis made on the American public and the media (radio, TV, newspapers) was virtually unparalleled in show business. If this was true, then certainly 1957 *belonged* to Jerry Lee Lewis. He exploded on the already turbulent pop music scene with the impact of an atomic bomb. Beginning with his frantic first appearance for Steve Allen, followed in rapid succession by three wild and crazy performances on Dick Clark's *American Bandstand* and a smash appearance in a major movie, *Jamboree,* Jerry Lee Lewis was the hottest act in show business. Every song he touched turned to gold. In an article which appeared in the late fifties, *Look* magazine commented: "Regarded as the ultimate in rock 'n' roll frenzy, Lewis makes parents mourn for the comparative quiet of Presley."

Many years later, in *The Rolling Stone Illustrated History of Rock & Roll* (1976), Peter Guralnick—in a story revolving around Elvis—wrote that "an egocentric genius like

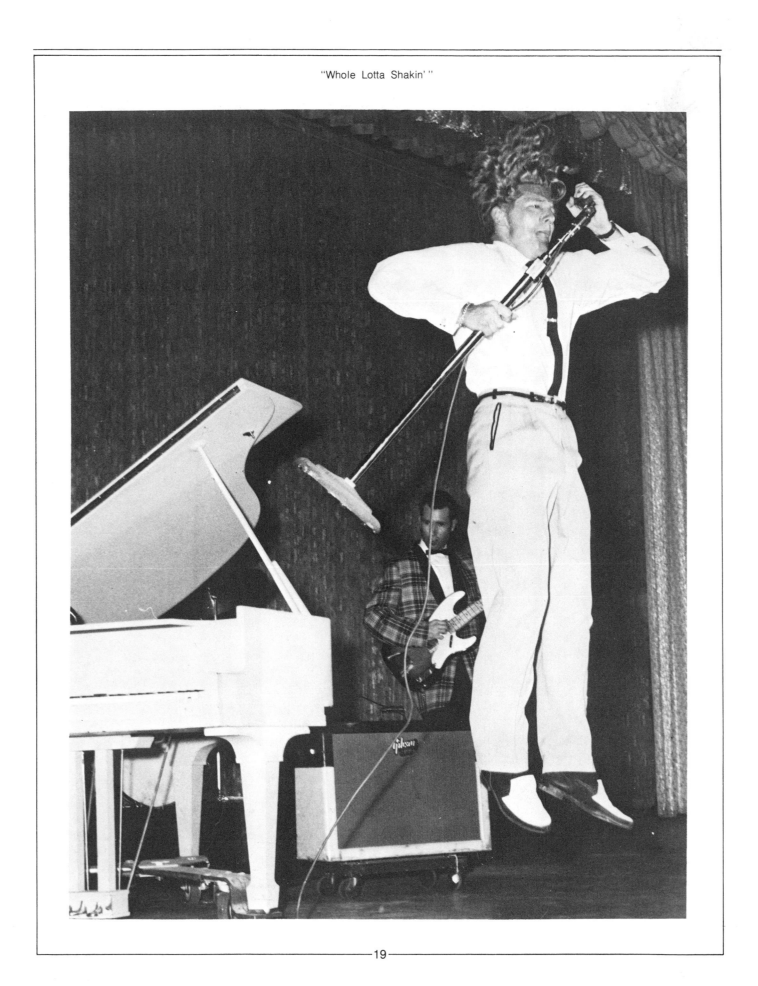

Kay Martin was the first president of the official Jerry Lee Lewis Fan Club, started in 1957. She appears here with Jerry Lee at Wildwood, New Jersey, in July 1959.

Gary Skala was the second president of the Jerry Lee Lewis Fan Club. This photo was taken at Keansburg, New Jersey, in July 1962.

Jerry Lee Lewis may even have had a greater talent."

January 8, 1958—Jerry's meteoric success story continues with his eighth appearance on a major television show—Patti Page's *Big Record.*

February 15, 1958—Jerry Lee Lewis performs his latest Sun single, "Breathless," on *Dick Clark's Saturday Night* [*Beechnut*] *Show*—another frenetic uptempo rocker also written by Otis Blackwell. Result: another million seller, his third in a row.

March 18, 1958—Jerry appears for the fourth time on Dick Clark's *American Bandstand.* Sings "Whole Lotta Shakin'," "You Win Again," and "Breathless" for a wildly enthusiastic audience.

April 1958—Making his eleventh major appearance on television in a ten-month period, Jerry Lee shakes Dave Garroway's

*Today* show with his rockin' version of "Down the Line."

Once again Hollywood beckoned young Jerry Lee Lewis. He appeared in his second major movie, *High School Confidential,* an MGM production which starred Mamie Van Doren, Russ Tamblyn, John Drew Barrymore, Jan Sterling, and Jerry Lee singing the title song from the back of a moving flatbed truck. The song, written by Jerry Lee along with Ron Hargrave, was another million seller.

Also in '58 Jerry appeared at the prestigious Paramount Theater in New York as one of the stars of a record-breaking *Alan Freed Show.* The crowds at this sold-out twelve-day engagement broke all previous attendance records for this theater (including ones set by Frank Sinatra and Johnnie Ray). In a recent interview (in *Genesis* magazine, July 1979) Jerry reflected on this record-breaking engagement.

*We were doing nine shows a day—twelve on Friday and Saturday. There were lines up for as long as twelve miles—they estimated from a helicopter, I'm telling you: you never seen anything like it!* The New York Times *came out and said Jerry Lee Lewis in the headline. Not Jerry Lewis or Dean Martin or Frank Sinatra or Patti Page or Desmond Decker. I got recognition. Fats didn't get recognition. The Everly Brothers. They all got mad. Fats said, "How come my damn name ain't in this thing?" "Your damn name ain't in there because you didn't close the show," I said. "You know you tried to close the show the first night, Fats." He said, "Yeah, I know. Dat's right." This was the greatest experience, and it will never happen again. The Paramount Theater on Broadway. They mobbed you and tore off your clothes, and you went in nekkid.*

Jerry Lee Lewis was on top of the world. At the age of twenty-two he had sold over *twenty million* records, he had appeared as a guest star on eleven major television shows, made two major movies, had four Gold Records in a row—he was king of rock.

# Trouble in Paradise

It might have all been for the best.
If I'd have kept going like I
was back then, I'd be dead by now.

Jerry Lee Lewis

In May 1958 Jerry Lee Lewis and his young bride, the former Myra Brown, flew to London on a thirty-seven-day tour to conquer England as he had conquered America. His fee for this concert tour was to be $100,000, which in 1958 would be considered a king's ransom. Accompanying Jerry Lee on his first overseas appearance were his sister Frankie Jean Lewis and Oscar Davis, his manager during this period.

Jerry's fame as a rock 'n' roll superstar had preceded him across the Atlantic. As the young honeymooners stepped from the plane, they were mobbed by members of the British press. Questions were fired at Jerry with machine-gun rapidity. Just as quickly, Jerry answered them: bluntly and honestly—the only way he knew how. Then the roof caved in.

Oscar Davis remembered the reaction to Jerry's teenage bride.

*They were shocked in England to see such a young girl. She looked about ten, you know, at that time, and we held a meeting at the Westbury Hotel, a press meeting, and everybody in England was there—everybody in the music industry—and everything was going fine. I stood with Jerry, and we talked to the various reporters, about twenty or thirty of them, and a friend of mine was in the audience, and I hadn't seen him, so I stepped aside, away from the reporters, and talked with Dick. In the meantime a couple of reporters broke away and they said, "Say, Davis, Jerry just said that he had been married four times," and so I said, "Oh no, he is kidding," and*

*so I stepped up and looked Jerry in the eye and said, "You're not—you didn't tell these people you had been married four times," and he said, "Yes, I have," and he started bang, bang, bang, bang—all the girls, you see. Now Jerry thought that, due to the fact that he was on an island, he had flown a great distance, that nothing that he said over there would mean anything over here, but it broke in all the papers over here—all the disc jockeys—and we had quite a furor. That was the beginning of a long slump of Jerry Lee Lewis.*

When the staid English press found out (from Jerry) that his bride was only fourteen and she was also his cousin and he was still married to another woman (Jane Mitchum) back in the U.S., the press had a field day. British papers headlined his marriage as "scandalous" and "shocking." British audiences booed his performances: after four days the tour was canceled. Back in the States even worse events were taking place.

Jerry and Myra returned to find that radio stations all over the country were banning his records. He had been blacklisted, and the ban continued for nearly ten years. For Jerry, the magic bubble of fame and fortune had burst, and the explosion made headlines all around the world.

More than anything else, he was a victim of his own inexperience. He was also a

With his bride, Myra, on their return from London, May 28, 1958.

prime target for the establishment backlash directed at rock 'n' roll music and anyone associated with it. Jim Sanderson, who later became a legal consultant for Jerry Lee, made this comment:

*Naiveté, I think, is the key word. . . . At the time I met Jerry, he had in the last eighteen to twenty-four months become a national figure. A man who espoused and artistically performed a very new, unique style of music which was acceptable, to say the least, all over the world. But he was not aware, and his advisors–if he had any prior to the time that I became involved with him—had not advised him or made him fully cognizant of what position he had reached in the entertainment world. As a matter of fact, on this trip to England, he and his young bride just simply stepped off the plane in full view of the photographers and newspapermen who, quite frankly, I think, scared him.*

In fact, marrying at a young age was not unusual for Jerry, who took his first wife, Dorothy Barton, at the age of fifteen. After a divorce, he then married Jane Mitchum at seventeen. They had one child, Jerry Lee

Lewis, Jr. (born February 11, 1954). Finally, in December of 1957, Jerry married Myra Brown, the daughter of J. W. Brown, a member of Jerry's band. So to be married very young was nothing exceptional, and the pubescence of Jerry's bride did not raise much comment in the South. Still, the reaction outside of that area was disastrous.

Jud Phillips, a close friend and business associate, commented:

*Well it was tragic—so cruel—to tear a man's career down because of his personal life. And this was a sincere act on Jerry's part: He really loved Myra, and it was his business. I think to a great extent maybe it was mismanagement, but it is really cruel when people will wreck your career and say that you're not capable of doing your job because you married a woman from across the tracks, so to speak. I am not insinuating that this is what happened in Jerry's case, but it was his personal life, and this was legitimate as relates to the law, and he was entitled to do so according to all the advice he had. I think it's real cruel, but on the other hand, Jerry took it like a man. I don't believe there is any other artist that could' have gone through what he has gone through and still retain his composure.*

Among those who witnessed the rise and fall of Jerry Lee was Dick Clark. In 1971 he explained:

*In the early days of rock 'n' roll, you've got to first remember that rock 'n' roll was an amalgam of country music and rhythm and blues music, both of which told the truth and, as we say, were a "right on" kind of music. It was right there, flat out in front of you. About drunkenness, adultery, doing your thing in bed—whatever. Things that in those days of America's being ever so naive weren't even discussed in public . . . to say nothing about sung about. The only time you'd ever hear them would be on*

*what we called in those days a race station. A black station, almost underground. (The same thing was true of a hillbilly station.) It's just another indication, I think, that America is older and sophisticated and ready to accept the facts of life.*

Oscar Davis remembers:

*Disc jockeys called me up and told me they were going to break all his records and everything, and they really mistreated Jerry. The disc jockeys over here, in England, the promoters—everybody. It was a horrible thing they did to him.*

At the same time that all of the negative publicity broke in the media, Jerry had just completed his second major movie, *High School Confidential.* Sun Records had just released Jerry's big single from the movie, which they had hoped would be his next Gold Record. It didn't quite work out that way. Bill Justis, who worked at Sun during those days, recalled the surprising effect of Jerry Lee's fall from grace:

*It was kind of hectic. I remember a lot of the distributors called up and wanted to return records: you know, because we had just released a record called "High School Confidential," and that was supposed to be a big "push" record—you know. It was at a real crucial point in Jerry's career, and I remember they sent an awful lot of 'em back. I think they sent back more than they sold, and then from there on out it was hard to get him played for quite a while.*

Still, Sun continued to release Jerry Lee's records. In 1971 Oscar Davis commented on the way in which he felt the situation should have been managed.

*I shouldn't have permitted Myra to make the trip, but I didn't have that much influ-*

With Myra, left, and his sister Frankie Jean Lewis, right, in London, May 1958.

*ence. You see, standing beside Jerry Lee Lewis and interfering with his relationship with everybody was Sam and Jud Phillips, the two Phillips brothers that had the Sun record label. Sam, knowing that Jerry was a very valuable property, fed him money constantly, bringing him big checks, and he, Jerry, could do no harm with them. Well, I wasn't producing the kind of income that they were producing on record royalties and advancing him money, so they had more control over him, and they were content to let Jerry bring Myra over.*

Many people in the music industry were of the opinion that if Jerry had had the benefit of the promotional genius of Colonel Tom Parker (Elvis Presley's manager), the entire episode might have been shrewdly manipulated to Jerry's benefit. Shelby Singleton worked with Jerry Lee after he left the Sun label (in 1963). In 1969 he purchased the Sun Record Company from Sam Phillips, including their legendary library of tapes featuring Jerry Lee Lewis, Johnny Cash, Carl Perkins, etc. When Shelby was asked if Colonel Tom Parker could have done for Lewis what he had accomplished for Presley, he gave this comment:

*I don't think so. The reason is . . . there's nobody can control Jerry Lee Lewis. And an act must be managed by a manager— the manager is the guiding force behind it. Actually, the artist or the act has to be directed and told what to do. Jerry Lee is the type of person that refuses to take direction, and he does exactly what he wants to do when he wants to do it. It's that simple; no matter who the manager would be with Jerry Lee—you can be his booking agent, or you can be his advisor—but in this business you could never be what we call a manager because he wouldn't listen to you.*

Even after the unfortunate publicity in 1958 put Jerry's career in musical limbo, the attacks on rock 'n' roll and its young disciples did not stop. Parents by the thousands were calling radio stations all over the country in a desperate but feeble attempt to stop the spread of this dreadful rock 'n' roll music that was corrupting the youth of America. State legislators introduced bills to ban rock 'n' roll from the airwaves. Preachers from their pulpits were denouncing rock 'n' roll as the music of the devil. Still it continued and grew bigger and bigger.

Not only did these audacious amateurs sing "black" music, these critics complained, but they looked strange with their greasy hair and long sideburns. If that wasn't bad enough, they had weird names like Elvis Presley, Conway Twitty, Fats Domino, Little Richard, Bo Diddley. Revolting, absolutely revolting, was the cry from white middle-class America.

The principal targets of this antirock parental hysteria were Elvis Presley, Jerry Lee Lewis, and Alan Freed.

Alan Freed became a primary target because he was the undisputed king of rock 'n' roll disc jockeys from 1954 to 1958. He pioneered the concept of low-budget movies featuring the top performers of the genre. *Rock Around the Clock; Rock, Rock, Rock;* and *Don't Knock the Rock* were just a few of the movies which spotlighted the talents of Little Richard, Bill Haley and the Comets, Chuck Berry, and Frankie Lymon and the Teenagers. Alan Freed is also credited with coining the term *rock 'n' roll.*

Elvis was singled out for intense criticism because of his "swivel hips" and the blatant sexuality of his onstage antics. When he performed on *The Ed Sullivan Show* in '57, the cameras were not allowed to stray below his waist.

Elvis was inducted into the army in March of 1958. He served two years like the "nice young boy" that he was, thereby escaping further criticism simply by being out of the country. Out of sight, out of mind.

Jerry Lee's marriage to his fourteen-year-old cousin Myra lasted for thirteen years and produced two children. Still, the public was outraged at this so-called "breach of morality." It almost destroyed his career.

When interviewed about his marriage and its repercussions, Lewis said,

*I was a twenty-one-year-old kid, and I didn't know whether I was comin' or goin'. But I don't regret any of it. If I had to do it, I'd do it again. I've got a lovely daughter I wouldn't take a zillion dollars for. So, therefore, I really came out a winner.*

When the world tumbled in on Jerry in 1958, one of the few who attempted to deal with the catastrophe was his manager, Oscar Davis.

*While I was in England, when all this controversy was going on regarding his marriage, I tried to clean it up the best I could and remarry him. I tried to marry him in France, but that's a highly Catholic country, and they wouldn't permit it. I tried to marry him in Ireland, and they wouldn't. I tried to get him aboard a plane and have the captain marry him, but the "law of the ship" doesn't apply to the captain of a plane. Then I tried to get him on a boat, going across the English Channel—have the captain remarry him: reestablish the thing so they didn't think he was living in sin with this young girl. That didn't work out. Then I went to the United States Consul [and] tried to get them to help us. They wouldn't help because it had received so much publicity by that time. On the exit from the Hotel Westbury we probably had two hundred reporters there with cameras and cameramen. The biggest exodus you've ever seen. When we finally got him on the plane, I breathed a sigh of relief—you know, to get him out of England. I was afraid he'd be harmed because they threw rocks and stones and everything at him. It was a horrible thing.*

One might wonder about the effect of all of this controversial publicity on a young, naive, twenty-two-year-old fellow from Fer-

# An open letter to the industry from JERRY LEE LEWIS

Dear Friends:

I have in recent weeks been the apparent center of a fantastic amount of publicity and of which none has been good.

But there must be a little good even in the worst people, and according to the press releases originating in London, I am the worst and am not even deserving of one decent press release.

Now this whole thing started because I tried and did tell the truth. I told the story of my past life, as I thought it had been straightened out and that I would not hurt anybody in being man enough to tell the truth.

I confess that my life has been stormy. I confess further that since I have become a public figure I sincerely wanted to be worthy of the decent admiration of all the people, young and old, that admired or liked what talent (if any) I have. That is, after all, all that I have in a professional way to offer.

If you don't believe that the accuracy of things can get mixed up when you are in the public's eye, then I hope you never have to travel this road I'm on.

There were some legal misunderstandings in this matter that inadvertently made me look as though I invented the word indecency. I feel I, if nothing else, should be given credit for the fact that I have at least a little common sense and that if I had not thought the legal aspects of this matter were not completely straight, I certainly would not have made a move until they were.

I did not want to hurt Jane Mitcham, nor did I want to hurt my family and children. I went to court and did not contest Jane's divorce actions, and she was awarded $750.00 a month for child support and alimony. Jane and I parted from the courtroom as friends and as a matter of fact, chatted before, during and after the trial with no animosity whatsoever.

In the belief that for once my life was straightened out, I invited my mother and daddy and little sister to make the trip to England. Unfortunately, mother and daddy felt that the trip would be too long and hard for them and didn't go, but sister did go along with Myra's little brother and mother.

I hope that if I am washed up as an entertainer it won't be because of this bad publicity, because I can cry and wish all I want to, but I can't control the press or the sensationalism that these people will go to to get a scandal started to sell papers. If you don't believe me, please ask any of the other people that have been victims of the same.

Sincerely,

*Jerry Lee Lewis*

This letter appeared in *Billboard* magazine on June 9, 1958.

riday, Louisiana. When questioned in 1971, Jerry Lee had this surprising comment.

*To be honest with you, it never really bothered me. I never changed. I just kept working. I lost a lot of popularity. I was making $10,000 a night at the time in '57, '58. That was like making $80,000 a night now, you know. So, I got knocked down from that to $250 and $300 a night. But it never bothered me.*

His attorney, Jim Sanderson, recalled that for many years thereafter,

*He really found it hard to rely on anybody's advice or anything other than his own intuition, in business matters at least. I know he became involved with back taxes with the Internal Revenue Department. (I handled these matters.) And Jerry found himself without any outlet for his ability as a performer. I was somewhat familiar with the business and I actually booked him into anyplace that we could get a performance date for him—for $250 a night in some VFW club in Arkansas or Mississippi. And this was the extent of Jerry's income there for a great period of time. He had no record royalties because the union, I think, had sort of put the quietus to that.*

Why did the musicians' union stop all of Jerry's royalty money? Because Jerry refused to perform at engagements that he had contracted to do, prior to his disastrous English tour. Jim Sanderson explained.

*After the England problem he had a great deal of trouble with the American Federation of Musicians. Now, this was due partly to Jerry's own naiveté. It was primarily because contracts had been lent by various booking agents for performances in various parts of the country, and, relying on these contracts, various promoters had rented various auditoriums, various halls,*

*and this sort of thing, but Jerry was so shocked, profoundly shocked, and so humiliated by this sort of intrusion into his private life that Jerry says, "Well to hell with them, I'm not going to go, I'm going to Louisiana and hunt. If they're going to interfere with my life, I won't play for them anymore," and consequently a number of promoters had their jobs blown. They had put out some, usually great, sums of money in advertisement, rental halls, and this sort of thing in which Jerry had contracted or had himself contracted to play, and Jerry just simply didn't show up. Again the key word is naiveté because I have always told him jokingly, "Jerry Lee, take you away from the keyboard and you really don't know where the hell you're at, do you?" And he admits to this.*

*He is becoming much more sophisticated today, however, and it's been a long road of hard knocks for him, but at that time, because he wouldn't make these contracted dates, of course, these promoters would file their claims within the organization established by the American Federation of Musicians, and these claims usually would run into thousands of dollars. So shortly after the England eruption Jerry found himself blacklisted or blackballed, as it were, by the American Federation of Musicians. They, claiming in behalf of promoters and other artists, that he had not fulfilled his contracts, and, therefore, they sent out the word in their own style that Jerry Lee Lewis—until he made himself right with the union and with these claimants—would not be allowed to perform freely.*

With the help of attorney Jim Sanderson, many of these complicated union problems were eventually resolved. But still it was a long, rough road ahead.

One person who had followed the rise and fall of Jerry Lee's career was Cecil Harrelson, who had grown up with him. Cecil explained how he went from a friend to the position of Jerry's road manager.

*When I started working for Jerry Lee Lewis, that was at his lowest ebb in his career, and he asked me, he says, "Would you like to go to work for me?" And I said, "Well, Jerry, I've got a good job, I've been with this company seven years." I said, "Well, I haven't anything to lose." You know, I was a young man, raised up with him. I said, "I'll go to work with you." I said, "I really don't know very much about the business." So I went to work for Jerry. I'll be honest with you. We was making a couple hundred dollars a day. We was playing just small joints. We worked, and Jerry was* *an electrifying entertainer, and he was an original entertainer, and he really had something on the ball. If the man hadn't had the talent to back him up, he would have been a dead artist. But he did.*

In 1960 someone at Sun Records came up with a brilliant idea. Jerry Lee recorded an instrumental number called "In the Mood." It was released on the Phillips International label (a division of Sun). The record was a strong, driving, boogie-woogie number with all the earmarks of a potential hit. To confuse the issue, the label read, "The Hawk," a pseudonym for Jerry Lee Lewis. This recording started to climb the charts rapidly; however, the minute the word

January, 1959: With his parents outside courtroom in Memphis, after testifying he was "about broke." Ex-wife Jane Mitchum Lewis charged he was behind $1,100 in alimony and child-support payments; the judge gave him one week to pay up.

leaked out that "The Hawk" was actually Jerry Lee, it was immediately yanked off the airwaves. The gimmick had failed.

Nineteen hundred and sixty-one was the year Jerry briefly broke into the charts. Back on the Sun label, his rockin' version of the old Ray Charles hit "What'd I Say" managed to get into the top twenty. It appeared that he was on his way back; however, that dream was short-lived. Subsequent releases failed to dent the charts, and the long dry spell continued.

As if Jerry had not suffered enough tragedy in his young life, on Easter Sunday, 1962, his three-year-old son, Steve Allen Lewis, was drowned accidentally in the family swimming pool. The infant had been named after Steve Allen, who gave Jerry his first network television exposure. It was a tremendous loss to both Jerry Lee and Myra. However, in 1963 (September 30, to be exact) Jerry and Myra once again became proud parents. Their daughter was christened Phoebe Allen Lewis and weighed seven pounds at birth. Phoebe was a beautiful baby with blue eyes and brown hair, and most people agreed that she favored Myra in appearance.

Now there was another mouth to feed, so back on the road went Jerry Lee and Cecil Harrelson, now his road manager. The jobs were becoming more frequent, and the fees were getting larger. Cecil Harrelson recalled,

*We worked small nightclubs and knock-down, drag-out joints and everything else. We worked, built a circuit up, and we got to where we was working fifteen to twenty days a month, and then we got up to twenty to twenty-five days a month, and we would make the circuit, pack these nightclubs, no record label backing us up at all. Man, we was doing it strictly on our own. I remember the first seven or eight years I worked for Jerry. Hell, I don't think I heard*

With Myra and newborn Steve Allen Lewis, born February 27, 1959.

*ten of his songs on the radio. That's just how bad it was.*

The year 1963 was important on the comeback trail for Jerry Lee. It was then that he left Sun and signed with Smash Records, a division of Mercury. Finally Jerry would be getting the publicity and promotion he needed so desperately to get his records aired. Shortly after signing with Smash, Cecil and Jerry Lee began to see a little light at the end of the tunnel. Cecil recalled it clearly:

*It started getting better in about 1964. We started climbing a little bit. We was getting our price up. We had a big nightclub circuit worked up. We, in fact, were playing all the days we wanted. We was working for $400, $500, $600 a day, and we just had a small band with us. Jerry had three pieces on the stage with him besides myself.*

From a television point of view, 1965 was clearly the biggest year for Jerry Lee Lewis since he first exploded on TV in 1957. During the period between January and September he made no less than nine appearances on the tube. He appeared on the *Lloyd Thaxton Show* (on January 1) and followed with a rockin' performance on a new show produced by Jack Good called *Shindig* (on February 17). Then the *Soupy Sales Show* (March 13), the *Clay Cole Show* (March 14), *Thank Your Lucky Stars* (England, March '65), again on *Shindig* (April 14), *Bruce Morrow's Go Go* (May 10), another appearance on *Shindig* (June 23) and finally a fourth shot on *Shindig* (September 23).

By 1967 it was obvious to many insiders in the music industry that the comeback of Jerry Lee Lewis was just around the corner. His records were being played frequently on the air, his numerous TV appearances were well received, and his price for a live concert continued to climb. And all of this had been achieved the hard way, without the benefit of a smash hit. In a moment of reflection, Jerry Lee recalled the long, hard struggle.

*Well, I'll tell you: I worked for ten years, didn't have a hit record, couldn't get a record played on the radio station. Everybody said, "No, ain't no way." I worked night-clubs, I built myself up from $250 to $300 a night up to $1,000 to $1,500 a night without a hit record.*

Cecil Harrelson comments:

*Jerry had some bad publicity and he did some things the public didn't like. If it would happen this day and age, people wouldn't think anything about it, but it happened back in an era, in a rock 'n' roll era, and they wanted to brand someone. Jerry Lee married a girl, she was young, she wasn't his first cousin, but still the newspapers and the magazines and everyone bloated it up and they jumped on it, and if he would have been handled right when he got all the publicity, he probably would have been the biggest artist that ever lived.*

There are many in the music industry who firmly believe that Jerry Lee Lewis *is* the "biggest artist that ever lived." Shelby Singleton has referred to Jerry Lee as "the world's greatest entertainer." Tom Jones, the English entertainer, called Jerry the number one rock 'n' roll performer of all time, and Nick Tosches, author of *Country: The Biggest Music in America*, has said that Jerry Lee may be "the greatest country singer alive."

# 4

# Mickey Gilley:
## An Interview

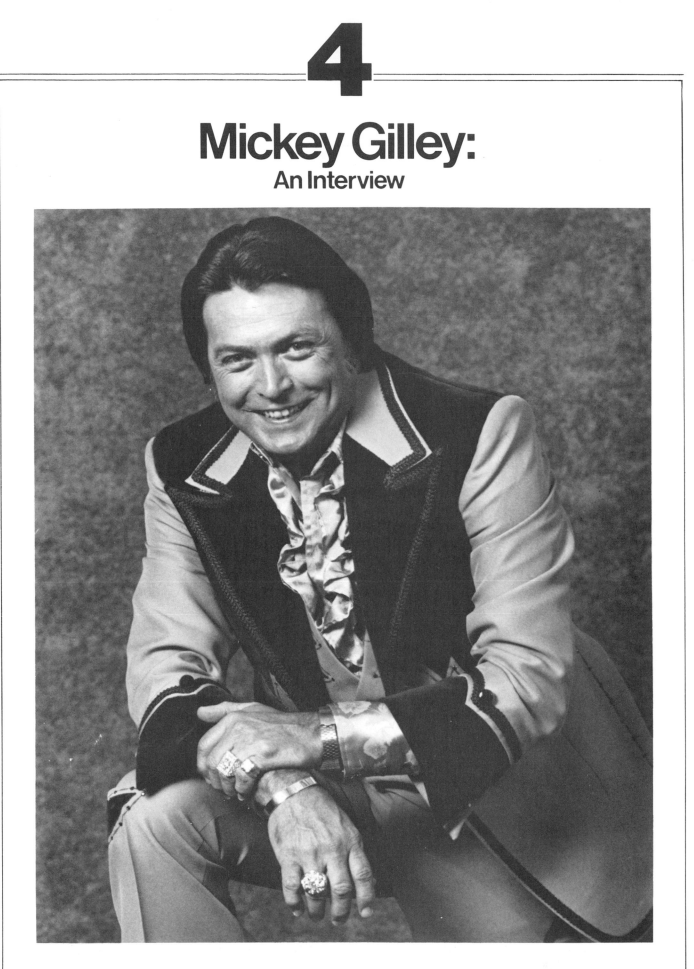

> I think that Jerry's music
> will live forever.
>
> Mickey Gilley

**A** successful record star in his own right with ten Number One country records to his credit, Mickey Gilley grew up with his cousin Jerry Lee Lewis in the typical small southern town of Ferriday, Louisiana. He shared Jerry's youthful dreams of becoming an entertainer; however, Mickey's dreams of success were not fully realized until 1974, when his disk "Room Full of Roses" went to Number One on the country charts. In 1977 he won the Country Music Academy award as "Entertainer of the Year." He also owns and operates Gilley's, a highly successful nightclub in Pasadena, Texas. The following interview took place in March of 1979.

**Robert Cain:**
How far back do you and Jerry go?

**Mickey Gilley:**
We were raised together in Ferriday. There is six months' difference between his age and mine. He was raised part of his life at Indian Village which is down in Clayton, and spent some of his time in Jonesville, Louisiana, which is some eighteen miles from Ferriday. Jerry and I used to hitchhike from Ferriday to Vidalia to go swimming because they had no swimming pool in Ferriday. Basically we were together all the way through the school years. I left for Houston when I was seventeen years old, and all the way up to that time we were associated as friends and cousins.

**Cain:**
What was Jerry like as a kid?

**Gilley:**
Well, Jerry seemed always to have a drive for music. I never pictured him doing anything else. Although I never dreamed he would become such a big star as he did in the fifties. As a kid he won many, many talent contests—in fact he won about every contest he entered. When Elvis hit, Jerry was working in Natchez, Mississippi. It was a small club, and if I'm not mistaken, I think it was the Wagon Wheel—anyway, he told me later another guy was playing piano and Jerry was playing drums. Jerry is a tremendous musician on drums, piano, guitar, or fiddle. He's very, very talented. I suggested at the time that he go to Memphis and talk to Sam Phillips because I knew of the success Elvis was having at Sun. The next thing I knew, when I came back to Ferriday from Houston, I found out that Jerry Lee had gone to Memphis. His mother gave me a copy of his first record called "Crazy Arms." I wish I still had it—it was a 78. The radio stations began to play "Crazy Arms" real heavy in the Houston area. The next time I saw him, a few months later, he told me he had a new song out called "Whole Lotta Shakin' Goin' On." They were not playing it in the Houston area because they thought it was too vulgar. Later he performed it at a concert, and within a matter of a week or so the song was

Number One in Houston. He was well on his way to becoming a national figure as far as rock 'n' roll music was concerned at that time.

**Cain:**
Did Jerry's parents want him to become a gospel minister, or was that his idea?

**Gilley:**
I would be speculating to tell you how his parents felt about that. I think Jerry has always felt he should have done what his cousin Jimmy Swaggart did and become a minister. Jerry feels he should have used his music to win other people into the church. Jimmy Swaggart is the only one of the three of us that became an evangelistic minister. I think Jerry feels his mother might still be alive today if he had lived the type of life she had expected. Jerry has taken a lot of things on himself and feels it is his fault that his mother passed away (he loved her dearly). He reminds me a lot of Elvis's situation. It bothers him a great deal: He feels he should have lived a Christian life instead of doing what he did with his music.

**Cain:**
Were you surprised when he became a big star?

**Gilley:**
I was very surprised. I never dreamed that someone in our family would achieve such national recognition. It was very exciting to see him on all the big television shows, especially when he appeared on *American Bandstand.* In those days that was the ultimate in becoming a star—to appear on Dick Clark's show. I was only associated with the Houston area music at that time. I didn't realize that there were national magazines like *Billboard* and *Cashbox* and that type of thing. I wasn't into it that heavy. But it was thrilling to see someone in the family achieve such great success.

**Cain:**
You recently did a show with Jerry Lee called "Pop Goes the Country." Was that the very first show you had ever done together?

**Gilley:**
Yes, that was the first time Jerry Lee and I worked together as far as television is concerned. I might say, it was one of the highlights of my career. Even though I have achieved some success in the country music field, it was a thrill to work with a man who had accomplished as much in music as Jerry Lee has. He made a lot of people sit back and say, "Hey, you know, these guys were raised together, and they are doing a similar style of music, and it's good."

**Cain:**
Is it possible you and Jerry Lee will record together in the future?

**Gilley:**
I have struggled very, very hard to get Jerry Lee to do an album with me. Not only do I think it would be good for Mickey Gilley, but I think it would be good for country music as a whole. Maybe I am reaching too far for something of that magnitude. It seems that everybody that was big in the rock 'n' roll era seems to be getting a lot of country music air play—like Waylon and Willie and Conway Twitty and people like that. Not that Jerry Lee really needs Mickey Gilley because he is such a well-known star. . . . .It would be great for country music. Jerry said he'd like to do it, but of course we have separate record companies to contend with.

**Cain:**
Is there any rivalry between you and Jerry, or are you friends?

**Gilley:**
I have always thought of Jerry Lee as a great personal friend. I couldn't think of anything that would come between us. For one thing,

I have always admired him and what he's done. When I go out to do a show and someone requests a Jerry Lee Lewis song and I know it, I'm going to do it. I know just about all of his hits because I used to sing them all the time. I don't do it to copy him; I do it because I admire him and what he's attained.

**Cain:**
Some people have said your style is too similar to Jerry's. Does this bother you?

**Gilley:**
Well, yes and no. For a long, long time I tried to change my style of music to get something I could achieve myself. But due to the fact that we were raised together and the boogie-woogie style of piano seems to be in our blood, I couldn't change what I had grown accustomed to. When my nightclub in Houston became a big success for me, I threw in the towel as far as my recording career was concerned. That's when I happened to cut "A Room Full of Roses"—a song that Jerry Lee and I used to sing when we were kids growing up together. A lot of people look back at "Room Full of Roses" and say it sounded like Jerry Lee, and they are right. I thought for a while it was a little too much like Jerry myself. But then I thought: What the heck, it will just be another local [Houston] record. Well, that's the record that hit big for me. As I look back now, I can see that I was trying to change what I was doing all the time in the clubs. When I became Mickey Gilley regardless of whether I sound like Jerry Lee Lewis or Jimmy Swaggart or Charlie Rich, it began to work for me. You've got to be yourself regardless of who you sound like.

**Cain:**
Many people refer to Jerry as a living legend. Would you agree with that definition?

**Gilley:**
There is no doubt about it. I think Jerry's music will live forever. I am very, very proud to have someone in the family that has attained the level of success that Jerry has in the music field. I don't think anyone will ever top "Whole Lotta Shakin'" or "Great Balls of Fire" or "Breathless." "You Win Again" I think is a classic. Definitely, he is a living legend.

**Cain:**
Could you give me some idea what Jerry Lee's mother was like?

**Gilley:**
She was my aunt: It's kind of hard for me to describe. She went to the Assembly of God church. She seemed to be a very loving, sweet person, as far as her kids were concerned, and basically, just a very caring mother. I don't know any other way to put it. She always seemed to care for her kids and her family . . . very deep convictions as far as her family was concerned. The times that I stayed with Jerry at his house, she was just like my mother was to me . . . very loving and caring.

I think Jerry Lee was probably closer to his mother than he was to his father. Also, Jerry has been very close to his family as a whole, including his sisters and his mother and his father. But I think he probably felt more for his mother than anybody.

**Cain:**
What was Jerry's reaction, generally, to Elvis?

**Gilley:**
Well, basically, I think that Jerry Lee probably enjoyed Presley's music, and I think he enjoyed the Beatles' music . . . although Jerry is the type of guy that I don't think really idolizes anybody. I think that he believes he is one of the best, and he believes that with all of his heart. Some of the things

that have happened in his career, he thought, probably shouldn't have happened to him. Deep down inside, I think, Jerry Lee thought and believed that he should have been in the position that Presley really was—that is strictly my observation, and I can't say that for a fact. I am just saying from what I've seen and what I've thought. I think that Jerry Lee felt that, since he played piano and was a stylist in his own right, that he should have gotten the publicity and the fanfare that Presley got and moved on up. A lot of things that Jerry Lee did probably hurt him—he would not let anybody take authority and direct his career. I think that if he'd have used somebody like Parker did with Elvis, I think that Jerry Lee would have been as big, or very close to Presley.

**Cain:**
Since Roy Orbison and Jerry Lee are now on the same label—Electra—do you think it's possible they might record together?

**Gilley:**
I don't think that Jerry Lee would ever record with anybody. I have talked to him about doing an album with him. . . . One day he says okay, and the next day I never hear from him—so I don't think Jerry is interested in recording with anybody, unless it's maybe his sister, Linda Gail, or somebody like that. I think Mickey Gilley would probably be the closest thing to him as far as recording [with somebody] is concerned.

**Cain:**
Does Jerry Lee have any hobbies or interests outside of his music?

**Gilley:**
When I talked to Jerry Lee last, I tried to get him to get interested in something other than what he had been doing in the last twenty years in the music field. I asked him about hobbies, and at the present time, from what I observed, he does not have any hobbies, other than piano playing and singing.

**Cain:**
Someone once said that Jerry Lee Lewis is the only entertainer who could star in a country show one night and the very next night he could star in a rock 'n' roll revue. Would you agree with that?

**Gilley:**
Yes, definitely. I would agree with that because Jerry Lee could do both sides of the field and do it expertly. One of the few people I've ever seen that could take a song and do it so many different ways that it would boggle your mind. I heard musicians in Nashville say that he was the only guy that they'd ever seen who could take a piano and get more out of three chords than anybody they'd ever recorded with.

With Sam Phillips, circa 1958.

# 5

# Sun Records Yesterday

> If I could find a white man
> who had the Negro sound and the
> Negro feel, I could make a billion dollars.
>
> Sam Phillips

The story of Sun Records is the story of rock 'n' roll. There are many who believe that without the incredible influence this tiny company wielded, and its amazing roster of successful artists, there would be no rock 'n' roll as we know it today. In the brief span of five years—1955 to 1960—Sun introduced six legendary artists to the musical world: Elvis Presley, Carl Perkins, Roy Orbison, Johnny Cash, Charlie Rich, and Jerry Lee Lewis. Under the guidance of Sam Phillips Sun gave birth to a brand new musical form: rockabilly, a unique fusion of black rhythm and blues and country music performed with wild abandon by young white artists. Rockabilly was born in Memphis but quickly spread across America . . . across the Atlantic . . . around the world. Twenty years later the echoes of the original "Sun sound" can be heard in the rock music of today.

Sun Records was the brainchild of Sam and Jud Phillips, who opened their tiny studio for business in the early fifties. The first commercial release bearing the Sun name was an alto sax duet with Johnny London playing lead saxophone, recorded on March 1, 1952. Sales for this initial release were disappointing, and the future for Sun looked uncertain. However, in 1953 Rufus Thomas's recording of "Bear Cat" on the Memphis-based Sun label enjoyed notable success in the rhythm and blues area. The follow-up "Tiger Man," once again by Rufus Thomas, did even better.

The success of these two rhythm and blues records enabled Sun to acquire national distribution in Memphis, New York, Los Angeles, and New Orleans. Jud Phillips recalls how it all began.

*My brother Sam and I were working at* WREC *radio station in Memphis, and we got to talking one day about all the people who were coming out of the Delta—like B. B. King, Muddy Waters, and people like that—that wanted to have dubs made so they could listen to themselves and maybe get records pressed. There was no place in the South where you could cut a record for commercial purposes, and finally we decided to open up a little studio at 706 Union and do custom work, and that's about the way it started. Then finally we went into producing and leasing the masters to Leonard and Phil Chess at Chess and Checker in Chicago. Then later on we decided, well, we'll just put out our own label and call it Sun.*

It was not until several years later—1956, to be exact—that Sun emerged as a major force on a national scale. The million seller "Blue Suede Shoes" was the record that brought fame and fortune to both Carl Perkins and Sun. It was in that same year that young Jerry Lee Lewis took his now legendary three-hundred-mile trip to the small red-brick building which housed the Sun studios.

Jud Phillips, who later was to become Jerry's manager, remembers the first time he saw Jerry Lee in action.

*I saw Jerry in a show—Johnny Cash, Red Sovine, Webb Pierce, and, I believe, Carl Perkins were in the show too—in Sheffield, Alabama, at the Community Center and he [Jerry Lee] was opening the show. He had a drummer and a bass player, I believe, with*

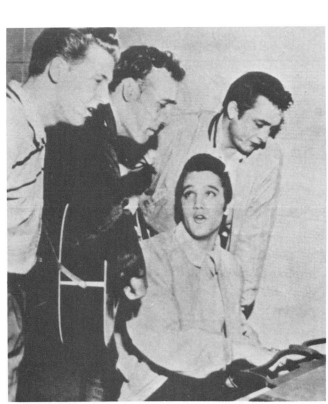

(Left to right) Jerry Lee, Carl Perkins, Elvis Presley, Johnny Cash: the "Million Dollar Quartet."

With Sam Phillips.

With Sam Phillips and his wife, Becky.

With the late Dewey Phillips, Memphis DJ, at a record shop.

Elvis Presley began his recording career with Sun Records.

Johnny Cash started with Sun and recorded there for three years.

Roy Orbison recorded with Sun from 1956 to 1958.

Carl Perkins recorded his huge hit, "Blue Suede Shoes," with Sun Records.

*him, and they were playing for $100 a night . . . and when I saw Jerry, I was really sold on him from the beginning. Well, he came to Memphis, and Sam, my brother, was out of town—he was down in Florida somewhere—and Jack Clement (after Jerry being very persistent) finally turned the tape machine on and let him sit down and audition. And after he heard it back, he said, "Well, my goodness. Look a here. Look what we got."*

The timing was perfect: Elvis had just walked out the door, and Jerry Lee had just come swaggering in. Sam Phillips had sold Elvis Presley's contract (and all existing tapes) to RCA Victor for some badly needed expansion capital. Any hopes of making a billion dollars on Elvis would have to be forgotten. Sam would have to settle for $35,000, which is all he received. However, in 1955 that was still a tremendous sum of money—unheard of for a singer with a lot of promise but as yet no track record. Sam was fully confident that he could create other rockabilly stars, just as he had made Elvis. It was a mere six weeks after Presley's departure that Sun came out with Carl Perkins's monster record, "Blue Suede Shoes." It proved to be the largest selling disc Sun had had up to that time.

Bill Justis was employed at Sun during much of their "golden" period (1957 to 1959). He recalls:

*In those days a little guy could start a record company, and if he got stuff that was selling along here and there—as long as he kept it selling—he could collect from distributors from what sold previously to the next hit. You stayed one hit behind with the distributors. There was a lot of excitement in the business. They had the personality disc jockeys, and the top forty format in radio was just getting started. In other words, you could cut a record and make a few phone calls to different big jocks (DJs) in different towns and just get them excited about it. Mail a dub of the record to their home: there were actually jocks that would take the things and play them all night. That kind of excitement is what really got rock 'n' roll going good. It was that personality disc jockey and, of course, that's all gone today. It's all automated now, like the supermarket and the calculator. But there were a bunch of those little record companies, and they're the ones that started giving the majors a lot of grief because the majors were so sticky they wouldn't go for this new sound, but they had the big checkbooks, and they could buy it. You know—like they bought Presley. If they wanted somebody, they'd go and buy him. A lot of times, when they got him, they didn't know what to do with him. It was a real strange thing.*

*This particular studio that Sam Phillips had, had a unique sound to it. And that wasn't because of sophisticated equipment, so much. They had a five-watt preamp that was made out of a kit. They had no echo chamber—all their echo was tape echo. They only had one power microphone: the rest were just regular old-fashioned-type RCA mikes. But for some reason this place got a unique sound*

*There were a lot of unique things about the place—it was a beehive of activity. You could go there at six-thirty in the morning—go there to listen to audition tapes, and get caught up—and people were knocking at the door. If they knew you were in there, they were waitin' outside to be heard. You could go down there on Christmas Eve day and there would be people there wanting to get in! The place was jumpin' . . . you know. The atmosphere was pretty weird because the floors were swept very sporadically. The venetian blinds on the two front windows of the building sagged. At any rate, the guys would come there and play their original songs—all of them wanted to record.*

*Maybe, out of every two hundred songs, you might tell one guy that this song has promise. ("Why don't you take it home and add some more lines to it and bring it back?") Well, a lot of those kids would quit their jobs and think they were stars! And if you told one of them you were going to record him, he'd definitely quit his job and go buy some old Cadillac from a bootlegger.*

*When Elvis went into the army, all of his sidekicks hung around there all day. We didn't have but a little bitty front lobby. . . . Well, it wasn't a lobby: I take that back. It was just a front office with one couch. There was people there all day long reading the trade magazines, and every once in a while they would go next door and get a cup of coffee. They'd talk the hip jive talk of the day about who's got the Number One record. It was really comical.*

*I don't know if the name Dewey Phillips means anything to you, but he had a lot to do with that company. He was the one that really got the Elvis records started there. He was the Number One personality disc jockey in the Memphis area. He was not related to Sam. Sam [Phillips] would take the records down there, and Dewey would put 'em on the air and play 'em and play 'em and play 'em again. He'd tell the people to call in and tell him what they thought. I know my record of "Raunchy": he broke that in the Memphis area in two days' time. He was a very powerful jock in that area. Of course, he loved the business, and he would come around Sun Records several times a week. He and Sam would often get into an argument. There was a lot of spirit, a lot of atmosphere. You could sit down and talk about it for days on end and never run out of conversation. It was some place.*

When I brought up the subject of Jerry Lee Lewis, Bill Justis had this comment.

*He always had a lot of . . . what you call "command presence." He would sit down and play, and everybody around would stop. He could actually get the floor away from Elvis. There were times when Elvis would drop in . . . late at night sometimes. One of them would sit at the piano and sing, and then the other one would go over there. Jerry Lee would always get people's attention over Elvis, believe it or not—and Elvis was big then! He's got that knack of getting people's attention.*

Sun's initial release by Jerry Lee was "Crazy Arms." It did well in the country area but did not make the national pop charts. His second record exploded. "Whole Lotta Shakin' Goin' On" was a song he had been doing for years in his stage act. He recorded it in one take.

"Great Balls of Fire" tore up the charts all over again. This was followed in rapid succession by "Breathless" and "High School Confidential." In the short span of two years Jerry had sold well over twenty million records. Sam Phillips's dream had come true. Here, indeed, was the white man who had captured completely the wild yet soulful sound of the black man. The man who was to make Sam Phillips a billion . . . well, maybe just a few million. Jerry is justly proud of the fact that he produced several Gold Records (million-sellers) on the Sun label—something that Elvis *never* managed to accomplish at Sun (he was there for sixteen months and released five different singles). The success of the Sun Record Company was related to Jerry Lee Lewis more than any other artist: He brought an incredible amount of worldwide attention to that minuscule label.

Jerry remained at Sun for seven long, highly productive years—longer than any other major artist discovered by Sam Phillips. He recorded hundreds of songs during this period (between four and five hundred), but most were never released because of the unfortunate negative publicity which stalled his career during the late fifties.

The first album Jerry Lee Lewis recorded, 1958.

**Jerry Lee's GREATEST!**

MONEY ● AS LONG AS I LIVE ●
HILLBILLY MUSIC ● BREAKUP
HELLO, HELLO BABY ● HOME ●
LET'S TALK ABOUT US ●
GREAT BALLS OF FIRE ●
FRANKIE AND JOHNNY
COLD COLD HEART ●
WHAT'D I SAY
HELLO JOSEPHINE

SLP 1265

His second album for Sun, 1961.

These Sun albums, released in 1971, 1978, and 1979, contain material recorded by Jerry Lee Lewis and others much earlier. The controversial *Duets* album, released in 1978, features vocals by a mysterious voice that sounds surprisingly like Elvis Presley.

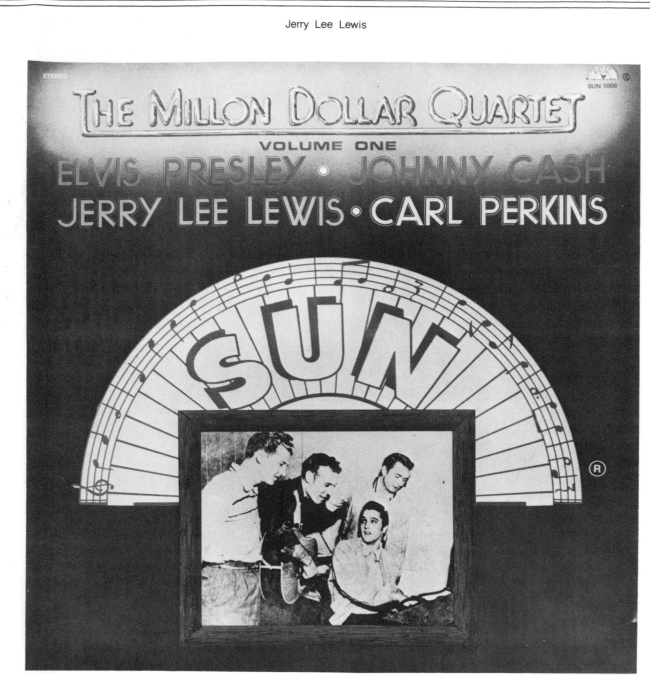

The famous "Million Dollar Quartet" album was recorded in 1957 and has yet to be released in the U.S.

Many factors played a part in the rise and decline of Sun Records as a major force on the music scene. The rise and subsequent fall from grace of Jerry Lee Lewis was one factor, but another was a change in the public's taste for rock music. The "hard rock" sound which Sun had helped make famous was being replaced by a "softer rock" sound in the early and mid-sixties. The "payola" investigations of 1960 shook up the entire music business but were directed principally at rock 'n' roll. Also, by the end of 1960, almost all of the major artists on the Sun label had left and moved on to other, larger companies.

Elvis Presley left the label to join RCA Victor after a brief sixteen months. Sun released five singles and no albums. His first release on Sun was "That's All Right (Mama)" backed with "Blue Moon of Kentucky" in 1954. It sold well in the South—about twenty thousand copies. In the Memphis area it rose to Number One on the country and western charts. His second single, "Good Rockin' Tonight," backed with "I Don't Care If the Sun Don't Shine," reached the Number Three position on the Memphis charts. Having gained confidence from his record sales, he auditioned for the Grand Ole Opry, where he was advised to stick to truck driving (he cried his way back home). At the end of 1955 Presley was proclaimed the "Most Promising Country and Western Artist" of that year. In late 1955 he had left Sun and in January of 1956 he had cut his first effort for RCA, which was "Heartbreak Hotel." The rest is history.

Johnny Cash signed with Columbia Records after three highly successful years with Sun (1955 to 1958). Probably his two most famous recordings for the Memphis-based label were "I Walk the Line" and "Ballad of a Teenage Queen." When interviewed in the early seventies, Bill Justis revealed an interesting story behind that recording.

*It was after "I Walk the Line," and they wanted to get some kind of new sound. So it was adding the voices, and we added piano and drums to him, and we had a monster hit called "The Ballad of a Teenage Queen." Johnny was mad at me for years for putting a soprano on his record because he couldn't emulate the sound when he went on the road . . . you know. But I guess he made some money out of it.*

Johnny Cash, along with Marshal Grant and Luther Perkins (known as the "Tennessee Two"), produced more than a dozen hit singles, which proved to be an important step in creating the unmistakable "Sun sound," a sound created by the unique styling of lead guitarist Luther Perkins and the deep, haunting voice of Johnny Cash.

Carl Perkins's million seller "Blue Suede Shoes" became the anthem for millions of teenagers during the mid-fifties. It was the first huge hit for the tiny label and must be remembered as the very first record to climb to the top in all three categories: pop, rhythm and blues, and country and western. Carl's career was tragically interrupted by a near-fatal automobile accident on March 22, 1956. The accident kept Carl out of the spotlight for many months and eventually claimed the life of his brother. Although Carl was a prolific songwriter and penned many notable tunes such as "Matchbox," "Honey, Don't," and "Bopping the Blues," none of these ever approached the tremendous popularity of "Blue Suede Shoes."

Charlie Rich rode his biggest record, "Lonely Weekends," into the pop charts in 1960 for the Phillips International label. It was his only big hit for them: however, he wrote many songs for other Sun artists, and his skillful piano styling can be heard on many records made between 1957 and 1960. Many believe his career at Sun suffered because he sounded too similar to Elvis and as a young man he even looked

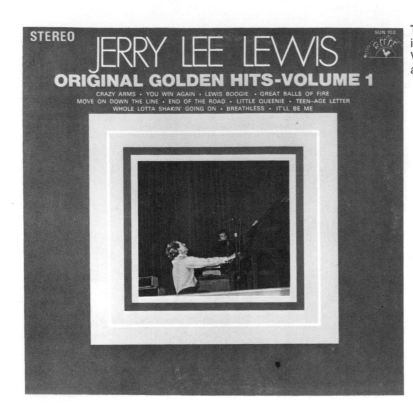

The "Original Golden Hits" series is a very successful one for Sun. Volume 1 is Sun's largest seller, according to Shelby Singleton.

STEREO

# JERRY LEE LEWIS
## ORIGINAL GOLDEN HITS
## VOLUME III

**SIDE ONE**
ONE MINUTE PAST ETERNITY
LET'S TALK ABOUT US
YOUR LOVIN' WAYS
I CAN'T TRUST ME IN YOUR
ARMS ANYMORE
LOVIN' UP A STORM

**SIDE TWO**
LOVE ON BROADWAY
SWEET LITTLE SIXTEEN
INVITATION TO YOUR PARTY
I LOVE YOU BECAUSE
AS LONG AS I LIVE
GOOD GOLLY MISS MOLLY

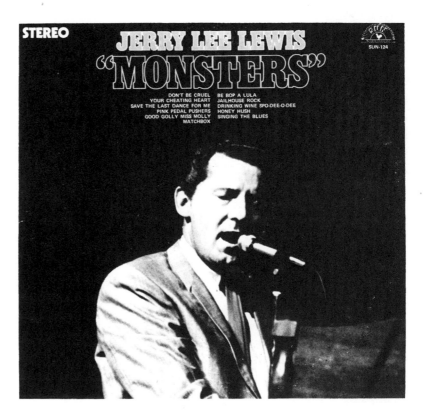

STEREO

# JERRY LEE LEWIS
## "MONSTERS"

SUN-124

DON'T BE CRUEL
YOUR CHEATING HEART
SAVE THE LAST DANCE FOR ME
PINK PEDAL PUSHERS
GOOD GOLLY MISS MOLLY
MATCHBOX

BE BOP A LULA
JAILHOUSE ROCK
DRINKING WINE SPO-DEE-O-DEE
HONEY HUSH
SINGING THE BLUES

like Elvis. In 1965 Rich joined the Smash label (with Sun graduate Jerry Lee Lewis) and produced another chart success in "Mohair Sam," written by Dallas Frazier. It was not until many years later on still another label that he finally achieved the recognition his eclectic talent deserved. Under the expert guidance of famed producer Billy Sherrill on Epic, he recorded "Behind Closed Doors," which in 1973 won the Country Music Association's award as "Song of the Year." Numerous hits followed, and today his music is widely acclaimed, and he is universally known as the "Silver Fox."

Roy Orbison's soaring bel canto voice was seldom exhibited during his brief stint on Sun (1956 to 1958). Sam Phillips attempted to make another rockabilly Elvis type out of this shy, young singer from Vernon, Texas. It didn't work, although Roy did manage one minor hit for Sun called "Ooby Dooby." By his own admission he always felt uncomfortable with the rockabilly style of material he was asked to perform. He had always considered himself to be a pure ballad singer. He left Sun to sign with RCA. Not long after, he moved to Fred Foster's young label, Monument Records. An accomplished songwriter, he composed tunes which were recorded by several top artists of that period: Jerry Lee Lewis ("Down the Line") and the Everly Brothers ("Claudette"). Roy also produced material for fellow Texan Buddy Holly. Orbison's million seller, "Only the Lonely," was the first of a long succession of smash hits on Monument which included "Blue Angel," "I'm Hurtin'," "Running Scared," "Crying," "Dream Baby," "In Dreams," "Mean Woman Blues," "Oh Pretty Woman," etc. Roy Orbison was right: he was a ballad singer.

Carl Mann was probably the last in the long list of promising young artists introduced by Sam Phillips. His disk of "Mona Lisa" topped the charts in 1959. Subsequent releases done in a similar fashion by this young singer and pianist—"Pretend" and "South of the Border"—failed to spark the same result. Although he became the second largest seller of recordings on the Phillips International label (Charlie Rich was first), he never again broke into the top forty.

By the mid-sixties Sun as an influential force was in decline, due much to the emergence of the Beatles and the following "British Invasion." In 1969 the legendary label was purchased by Shelby Singleton, Jr.

Under new ownership Sun began releasing much of the valuable vintage material which had been overlooked or ignored by Sam Phillips. Simultaneously on his new label (Mercury) Jerry Lee was finding great new success as a country crooner. Capitalizing on Jerry's renewed popularity, Shelby Singleton finally released the vast number of recordings which had been shelved during Lewis's decline. The results were surprising, to say the least.

One after another the "new" disks shot up the country and western charts. First came "Invitation to Your Party," Number Six; then followed "One Minute Past Eternity" (Number Two); "I Can't Seem to Say Goodbye" (Number Six); "All Around the Water Tank" (Number Eleven); "Love on Broadway" (Number Thirty-one). Jerry found himself in the position of being a smash on two different labels at the same time.

In addition to the great sales of the singles, there was a fantastic response to Jerry's albums—*Jerry Lee Lewis Original Golden Hits*, volumes 1, 2, and 3, *Golden Cream of the Country, A Taste of Country, Monsters,* and *Rockin' Rhythm and Blues.* Sales on these rockabilly gems went into the hundreds of thousands.

"The Killer" and Buddy Holly.

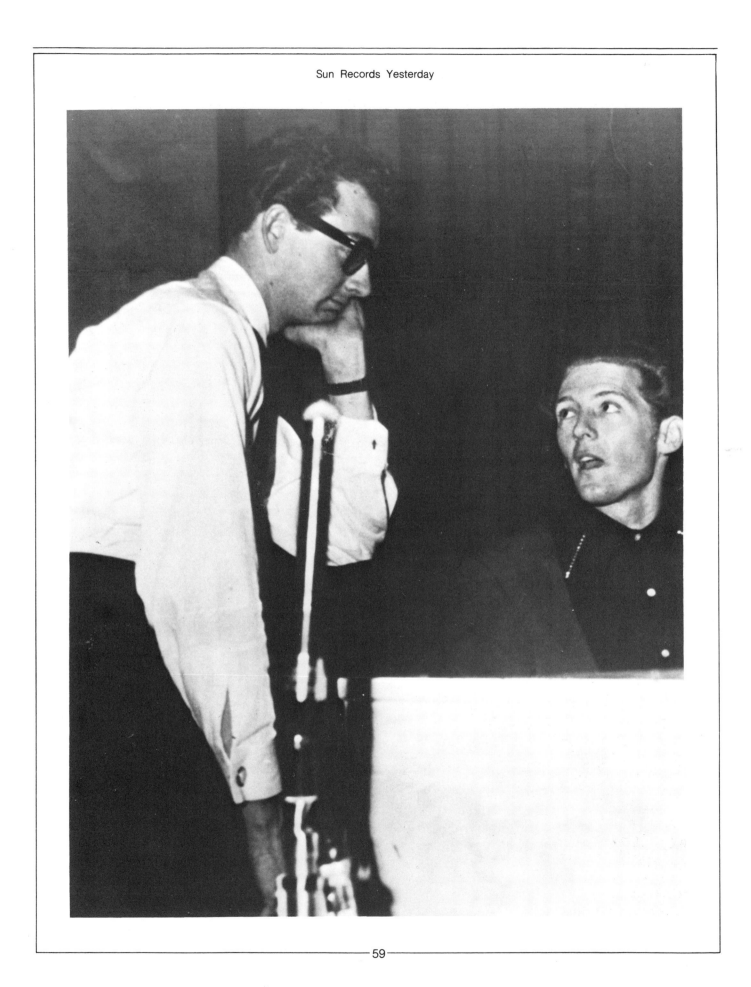

# 6

# Steve Allen:
## An Interview

> I've had some hard times,
> but you'll never find a business
> as good as this one. I tell
> people at every show that I
> love them, and I do. I give them
> everything I've got.
>
> Jerry Lee Lewis

**W**ith his jovial, bespectacled face and rapier wit, Steve Allen has been a favorite on American television screens for over thirty years. Starting in 1950, he starred in a number of early evening and daytime shows, made the guest circuit of *This Is Show Business* and *What's My Line,* and for over a year emceed a weekly series called *Songs for Sale.* In 1954 NBC had a title, "Tonight," and ninety minutes of air time. They gave it to Steve Allen, and within a year he had developed the show into a national institution. In 1956 he began an hour-long comedy variety show opposite the mighty Ed Sullivan. For many months Allen was doing both the ninety-minute *Tonight* show nightly and the sixty-minute *Steve Allen Show* on Sunday. Eventually, the pace proved to be too much for him, and he decided to give up the *Tonight* show and suggested to NBC that Jack Paar would be an excellent replacement. The prime-time *Steve Allen Show* continued for another four years, and the rating duels between the Ed Sullivan and Steve Allen shows became legendary. In 1960, having won the Peabody Award for the best comedy show, he bowed off the network after seven years with NBC. Allen then began a weekly comedy hour on ABC–TV in 1961–62. The following year he returned to his old *Tonight* show formula for Westinghouse, which continued nearly three years. This was followed by three seasons as the host of *I've Got a Secret.* In 1976 he scored again with another comedy format titled *Steve Allen's Laugh-back,* a weekly ninety-minute program reuniting many of his old "gang" in highlights from past memorable shows. His unique hour series *Meeting of Minds* marked another highlight in his remarkable career in 1977. What with the *Tonight* show, the Sunday night *Steve Allen Show,* and his numerous other programs, many of today's most famous stars received their first (or most important) TV exposure from Steve Allen. Some of these are Steve Lawrence, Eydie Gorme, Andy Williams, Pat Harrington, Jr., Louis Nye, Don Knotts, Tim Conway, Don Adams, Bill (José Jiminez) Dana, Jack Jones, Jonathan Winters, Lou Rawls, Jim Nabors, Mort Sahl, Peggy Lee, the Muppets, the Supremes, Helen Reddy, Steve Martin, Brenda Lee, Judy Collins, and Jerry Lee Lewis. In the following interview (from October 1979) Steve discusses Elvis Presley, Jerry Lee Lewis, and the music of the fifties.

**Robert Cain:**
What were your first impressions of Jerry Lee Lewis when he appeared on your show in July of 1957?

**Steve Allen:**
I remember him as a very exciting, energetic performer, who was noted for his jumping around and standing up while playing the piano, and that sort of thing. I recall that while he was doing one of his numbers on the show—it might have been "Great Balls of Fire" or "Whole Lotta Shakin' " or one of those exciting boogie-woogie sort of

*The Steve Allen Show,* 1957. (Left to right) Joanne Gilbert, Jerry Lee, Steve Allen, Dennis Day, Louie Nye, Tom Poston, Don Knotts.

things—he got the joint jumping so much that, since ours was chiefly a comedy show (in contrast to *The Ed Sullivan Show*), I grabbed a chair that was on the side of the stage. I saw the director had sort of a wide shot, and I just slid the chair right through the picture. And I think I threw my hat or something through the picture, to add to the general craziness..

**Cain:**
In 1957 Jerry Lee appeared on *The Steve Allen Show* three times in a row. Wasn't that rather unusual?

**Allen:**
Yes, it was. That might have been something

that was suggested by the network or occurred to our producer to suggest. I generally concentrated on the comedy aspects of the show. Although, because we were on opposite Ed Sullivan, we were under constant pressure by NBC to book people who were "hot box office" on the show—whether they had hit a home run or something of that nature: the same sort of thing that Ed Sullivan did. We had the early experience with Elvis, who was on our second show and who got us a very big rating, higher than Sullivan's rating on that occasion. All the networks care about is ratings. They expected we'd do a good show, but they wouldn't care if you did a *lousy* show as long as you had a good rating. Jerry had a hit record at that point, and I guess they figured by booking him three times, some sort of momentum might build up.

**Cain:**
Were Elvis and Jerry Lee Lewis similar or, to the best of your recollection, totally different personalities?

**Allen:**
No two people are exactly the same. They had some factors in common. They both were country boys. They both seemed nice and friendly. I never really got to know either one intimately. When you work on a show together, you're so busy doing the show . . . . (You might have lunch at a restaurant across the street or horse around during rehearsal, but it's not like going on a fishing trip with a guy where you really get to know him.) All I can remember, at this late date, is Jerry Lee being a very pleasant guy. I have an Arizona background myself, so I'm closer to country people than the average entertainer who might have been raised only in New York or Chicago or something of that sort. Some of my old Arizona friends are still good friends of mine. That may or may not have anything to do with my liking both Jerry Lee Lewis and Elvis.

**Cain:**
There were certain subtle restrictions on Elvis when he appeared on your show that did not seem to apply to Jerry Lee. Why was that?

**Allen:**
Yes, I think that since Jerry Lee was on the show after Elvis, that particular issue had pretty much evaporated. I mean the whole controversy on editorial pages and in church sermons and that sort of thing about Elvis and his wiggling around. It was that controversy about Elvis that first came to public attention. Since ours was primarily a comedy show, we just didn't put Elvis on

and let him go . . . the way Sullivan did. I dressed him in white tie and tails, I had him sing "Hound Dog" so we got this basset hound and set it up on a Greek column. The stage was set up as if he was going to do a reading in the manner of Charles Laughton or Laurence Olivier. Very dignified and classic. So in that case with Elvis the point was to get laughs and still let him sing whatever he wanted to sing. Whereas sometime later, when we had Jerry Lee on the show, that no longer was an important question, so we just got out of his way and let him do his own thing.

**Cain:**
Being a pianist yourself, what was your impression of Jerry's rather unorthodox style of piano?

**Allen:**
I do recall that I was surprised that he was as good a pianist as he was. I hadn't been intimately familiar with him, except by recordings before that, and you can't see anybody on a record. I hadn't known before he worked on my show that, in addition to being a singer, he was also a good piano player. I have a recollection that he played in a boogie-woogie style. These days, when I do my own nightclub or concert act, I do one boogie-woogie number. My whole show is pretty much oriented toward jazz, and I explain—if there are an appreciable number of young people in my audience—that there's a lot of good instances of music in the rock 'n' roll category, but that they shouldn't make the mistake of thinking it just started about eight or nine years ago—or last week, for that matter. I say: "I would like to play for you now a kind of music that was old stuff even in your father's generation. This is from the 1920s, in other words, from your grandfather's time." Because that's when the first Pinetop Smith and that sort of boogie-woogie stuff was played. So it's a good authentic musical form, and Jerry Lee played it very well.

**Cain:**
What was your reaction when you learned that Jerry had named one of his children, Steve Allen Lewis, after you?

**Allen:**
I was *very touched*. You always see yourself in a certain way, you know, in the mirror when you shave in the morning. To yourself, you are just you. In that sense, I'm sure that the most important man in the world, when he's in the shower, he's no big deal to himself. You only get that sense about yourself when you're onstage and twenty thousand people are screaming for you, or if you see your picture on *Time* magazine. So whenever there is any public compliment of that sort, my initial response to it is surprise and then a certain sense of pleasure. I remember being very touched by that.

**Cain:**
Jerry's career was almost wrecked by his marriage to a fourteen-year-old girl. What are your thoughts on that?

**Allen:**
I guess most people would disapprove of that. But I know people who are thirty who are still immature. I know some women at thirty who seem like they ought to be in the eighth grade. I can recall having met a few girls of fourteen or fifteen, over the years, who seem as mature as twenty-year-olds. Not having known the girl, I couldn't make any more critical comment about it. But I

*The Steve Allen Show,* 1957.

can understand that it is the sort of thing that would seem scandalous to certain people. However, you would have to relate it to the social situation in the southern states, the Bible Belt states, the areas where country music is dominant. According to some scholarly studies I have come across, the mother of Jesus was only about fourteen or fifteen when he was born, and no one is scandalized at that. At that time, two thousand years ago in that part of the world (and for that matter even now), it is normal for young women to marry at that age. Apparently, if they get to be twenty, they feel like we would at forty—an old maid, or something. So again, I don't know at what ages people commonly get married in Mississippi or Alabama—

**Cain:**
In those areas, it's common to marry young.

**Allen:**
Well, then it was no big deal.

**Cain:**
Certain performers seem to evoke a hysterical reaction from an audience. Elvis had this quality, Jerry Lee has it, and so did Johnnie Ray.

**Allen:**
Yes, there are certain performers that have a certain appeal to teenagers, not to put them down—or up for that matter. . . . Frank Sinatra did when he was a young guy. I'm not sure why that is. With rare exceptions, it's

singers that produce that reaction. No one ever reacts that way about the world's greatest comedians. As great as Groucho Marx was, or Charlie Chaplin, no one ever screamed for them—they just laughed at them. It rarely even happens for actors. There are some actors who are in the matinee idol category like Clark Gable (and I'm sure there must have been some situations when he was trying to get from a restaurant into a car and a few women squealed when they saw him), but the real mob hysteria happens only with singers. It must have something to do with the fact that their art form is the musical form, and I think it has to do with a kind of immature music. In other words, music which speaks directly to the sixteen-year-old audience. It wouldn't happen to an opera singer who, let's say, is much more talented and sings more important music: no one would ever go crazy trying to tear his clothes off outside a restaurant. I know, having been through the teenage years myself, music is very important to you at that age. You are open to all sorts of emotional input. You are emotionally much more sensitive than you are later in life. If you were to ask the average fifty-year-old man what songs were most important to him, ask him to name the ten songs that really touch him, he will in almost every case mention the songs he dug when he was fifteen to twenty-five years old. That's true of all of us.

In the case of rock people such as Elvis, Jerry Lee Lewis, and others, the music itself has a very infectious beat, so there's the kind of excitement that music provides. I think there may be five or six factors all combined, to explain that kind of hysterical reaction. One of the factors has nothing to do with whatever they are screaming about; it's all within the audience. There are formal studies of mob psychology or mass psychology, some of which are very unpleasant historically. The witchcraft crazes . . . The Crusades were another example of mass hysteria. There have been many instances down through history. Sometimes they can have light and pleasant connotations, such as screaming for a singer or something of that sort. But what is involved is that same emotion of mass hysteria which can produce good results or evil results.

**Cain:**
The period of the fifties has been called a unique chapter in popular musical history. Would you agree with that?

**Allen:**
Yes. Of course, most of the periods are not divided sharply by the decades: Music doesn't suddenly change Monday morning, January first of 1960. But there are demonstrable differences from one period to the next, and some crazes or fads do last for approximately ten years. It's typical that these various musical periods are distinct or differentiated from all the others. There were some good things about the music of the fifties and also some bad things. It was the first period when the national audience—which consisted chiefly of young people, in terms of buying records and sheet music—turned away from the heretofore acknowledged masters in the art of creating music, as distinguished from singing it (by that I mean Cole Porter, Richard Rodgers, George Gershwin, Johnny Mercer: you know, people of that sort).

**Cain:**
You mean songwriters like Hoagy Carmichael?

**Allen:**
Yes, Hoagy Carmichael, Jerome Kern, Harry Warren. These people and a few others had created music of really remarkably high quality, in most cases. They had set the standard, and what suddenly happened—I think it happened partly on the street and then got reflected in the record business—

was that young people began to come along who, for whatever reasons, didn't know anything about these great masters and just began to learn to play the guitar, or maybe the piano a little bit, knew only a few chords, and began writing their own kind of songs. Some of those songs turned out to be catchy and listenable and worth remembering. A lot of them, the truth must be stated, were incredible trash. Now there had always been trash in popular music and there always will be. During the great period of the thirties and forties, not every song was an Irving Berlin masterpiece—there was always garbage. But there never was *that* kind of garbage before.

It was a brand new kind of trash. Characterized by an awfully high incidence of the word *baby* and the word *yeah* and a kind of a harmonic monotony. One type was the teenage stuff, which even now guys as talented as Paul Anka or Neil Sedaka apologize for having written. Then there was the Beach Boy trash: When they got through their trash period, they came up with some pretty good stuff. So the basic talent was there. One of the reasons why some of these relatively inferior songs became popular was through an accident of cultural fate. Rock music as a cultural form became popular. Of course, it was not invented by any of the white singers. In the thrities and forties it was called rhythm and blues, and there were two divisions of that. There was the big band black Kansas City or Chicago or New York type music, which in itself was kind of a switch from the swing type music of Count Basie, Fletcher Henderson music played in the thirties. But then, so many blacks were rural people, especially from the South. . . . That factor eventually influenced the form, so some of the music became more simple.

Then along in the early fifties, to get back to that period, some of the white guys began singing in that style and began adding their own creative additions to it. Rock music is wonderfully infectious rhythmically. For ex-

ample, when you play "Stardust," you realize that happens to be a good song, and if someone wrote a song in that form that was lousy, you would immediately know it was lousy. But in the case of rock, some of the garbage is easily disguised because that *rhythm* is so terrific. Your body so enjoys what the guitars are doing and what the drummers are doing and the syncopation and the musical accents that you can really take an innocuous tune and have a lot of fun with it. That's what happened with some of the things that Elvis recorded, and I'm sure it happened in the case of Jerry Lee and all the other rock singers. It will happen next week too; it's still going on.

**Cain:**

You have introduced so many successful performers on your shows: Steve Lawrence, Eydie Gorme, Andy Williams, Jack Jones, the Supremes, Peggy Lee, Jerry Lee Lewis, etc. Is there any particular quality you look for?

**Allen:**

There is no one quality, no. But I am more sensitive to talent than either the average talk show host, or for that matter, the average producer, writer, or television executive. Not that I am in any way inherently superior to my co-workers in the business, even on this point. It's purely a matter of early conditioning. My mother and father were vaudeville entertainers, so I grew up hanging around theaters. By the time I had to go to school—at six or so—some of that stopped, but not completely. During summers I would still hang around theaters. I began entertaining myself in school and that sort of thing. Now, if my father had owned a garage, today I could listen to your car and tell you what was wrong with it. We all learn about the neighborhoods we grow up in. So that's all there is to the so-called "secret" of why I've discovered fifty-two or fifty-three of the people that have become very big in the business. Generally, I could just see them or hear their record (or see them in a nightclub, wherever they are) and right away tell that they are talented. There have been some instances when I didn't have to make such a judgment. That would be the case regarding Jerry Lee Lewis. I didn't discover him in some little dive in Macon, Georgia. He was already making good records, and the records were hits, and that's what led to our booking him.

**Cain:**
Could you offer any explanation why Jerry Lee Lewis has remained a star for nearly twenty-five years, while many of his contemporaries have vanished?

**Allen:**
No, I doubt if I can. There is never anything scientific about the arts. The arts are very largely a matter of judgment. There are people sometimes without dazzling talent who become popular; there are others who seem to be very talented, who for whatever reason never quite get that big break, that certain hit record, that major television exposure. Generally, when people do remain popular over a long period of time, they can't be faking it. Jerry Lee obviously has something that communicates itself to audiences. There are performers who do not have a great deal of talent but nevertheless luck out with some early hit records or one hit record. They can coast along on that for a while. Then, suddenly, you can see when you book them into a club, nobody shows up anymore. But in the case of Jerry Lee Lewis, the audiences have been showing up for a good many years.

In *High School Confidential*, 1958.

# 7

# The Movies

In 1956 *Rock Around the Clock* started the trend of featuring prominent rock acts as the focal point of a film—against an embarrassingly naive plot. This picture featured Bill Haley and the Comets, the Platters, and the reigning king of the DJs, Alan Freed. Afterward, movies would never be the same.

Shortly after the film's release, numerous theaters where the movie played told wild stories of riots, vandalism, dancing in the aisles, and fist fights. Many cities attempted to have the film banned from further exhibition. Partly as a result of the extensive newspaper publicity these riots received, the picture shattered box office records everywhere. Hollywood was quick to sense a bonanza in the making and hastily whipped together three more low-budget rock 'n' roll quickies: *Shake, Rattle, and Rock; Don't Knock the Rock;* and *Rock Pretty Baby,* also released in '56. All of these quickie productions cleaned up at the box office. Now virtually every rock performer of note was called to Hollywood to perform in one or more of these hastily produced rock 'n' roll extravaganzas. For at least the next ten years Hollywood continued to ride the rock 'n' roll bandwagon.

Jerry Lee Lewis appeared in no less than six of these cinematic rock productions, starting with *Jamboree,* in 1957, *High School Confidential* in 1958, and finally *American Hot Wax* in '78. If frequency of appearance on television is any criterion of popularity, then *Jamboree* and *High School Confidential* must qualify as minor classics. *American Hot Wax* was a surprisingly accurate portrayal of the tragic decline of the "father" of rock 'n' roll, Alan Freed.

*Jamboree*       1957
(Musical)

WARNER RELEASE of a Max J. Rosenberg-Milton Subotsky Production. Director, Roy Lockwood; screenplay, Leonard Kantor; editors, Robert Broekman, Anita Posner; sound, Warren McGrath; music, Niel Hefti.

CAST: Features Fats Domino, Jerry Lee Lewis, Jimmy Bowen, Buddy Knox, Charlie Gracie, Count Basie and Orch, Joe Williams, Jodie Sands, the Four Coins, Frankie Avalon, Lewis Lymon and the Teenchords, Slim Whitman, Andy Martin, Carl Perkins, Ron Coby, Rocco and His Saints, Kay Medford, Bob Pastene, Paul Carr, Freda Holloway, Dave King-Wood, Jean Martin, Tony Travis, Leonard Schneider, Aaron Schroeder.
PREVIEWED November 12, 1957. Running time: 85 minutes.

"Jamboree" was filmed apparently with a single objective—to present a parade of stand-up singing talent. Film is dated in concept, reminiscent of the early days of musical films when producers slapped a group of singing acts together, but is okay for programmed situations where younger patrons like their vocals stylized, and particularly the jukebox trade.

Acts in the Max J. Rosenberg-Milton Subotsky production are strung together via a loosely contrived story line of two young singers falling in love, then splitting through the machinations of boy's ambitious femme manager. Producers use the device of having twenty-one DJs throughout the U.S. and Canada intro various entertainers. Such art-

*Jamboree,* 1957.

ists as Fats Domino, Count Basie, Jerry Lee Lewis, Jodie Sands, Ron Coby, Slim Whitman, Charlie Gracie, and the Four Coins head the entertainment section in rock 'n' roll, rockabilly, swing, and romantic rhythms.

Paul Carr and Freda Holloway team as the youngsters beset with romantic complications, both scoring nicely in roles and duetting with "Who Are We To Say" and "Twenty-Four Hours a Day," clicky songs each. Kay Medford and Bob Pastene are good as their respective agents, formerly wed, but now going their own separate ways, windup showing them clinching again. Dave King-Wood is okay as a label head.

Most of the acts are staged against either a telethon or Music Operators of America convention setting. Fats Domino comes through best with "Wait and See," Ron Coby handles "Toreador" nicely, Slim Whitman makes the most of "Unchain My Heart and Set Me Free," and the Four Coins warble "A Broken Promise." Jodie Sands also is good with "Sayonara." Other artists include Frankie Avalon, Carl Perkins, Jimmy Bowen, Buddy Knox, Joe Williams (with Count Basie), Andy Martin, Lewis Lymon and the Teenchords.

Roy Lockwood's direction of the Leonard Kantor screenplay is standard. Niel Hefti's musical score and direction satisfactory, and Jack Etra's lensing okay.

Whit.

Reprinted courtesy of *Variety*

## High School Confidential 1958
### (Teener Dope Meller)

METRO RELEASE of an Albert Zugsmith Production. Director, Jack Arnold; screenplay, Lewis Meltzer and Robert Blees; from a story by Robert Blees; camera, Harold J. Marzorati; editor, Ben Lewis; art direction, William A. Horning, Hans Peters; sound, Dr. Wesley C. Miller.

CAST: Stars Russ Tamblyn, Jan Sterling, John Drew Barrymore; "guest stars" Mamie Van Doren, Ray Anthony, Jackie Coogan, Charles Chaplin Jr.; with Diane Jergens, Burt Douglas, Michael Landon, Phillipa Fallon, Lyle Talbot, William Wellman, Jr.
PREVIEWED at the studio, May 21, 1958.

"High School Confidential," the first of Albert Zugsmith's productions for Metro since his moveover from Universal, is a sensational account of pills, marijuana, and narcotics among the high school set. A good cast, headed by Russ Tamblyn and Jan Sterling, does a capable job of projecting the sad and sordid aspects of this kind of story. Although the presentation seems to exploit to the fullest every facet of this evil situation, it does so skillfully and with compelling effect. "High School Confidential" will undoubtedly be a big box office success for its type.

Unknown to fellow students at Santa Bello High School—and to the audience for much of the film—Russ Tamblyn is in reality an un-

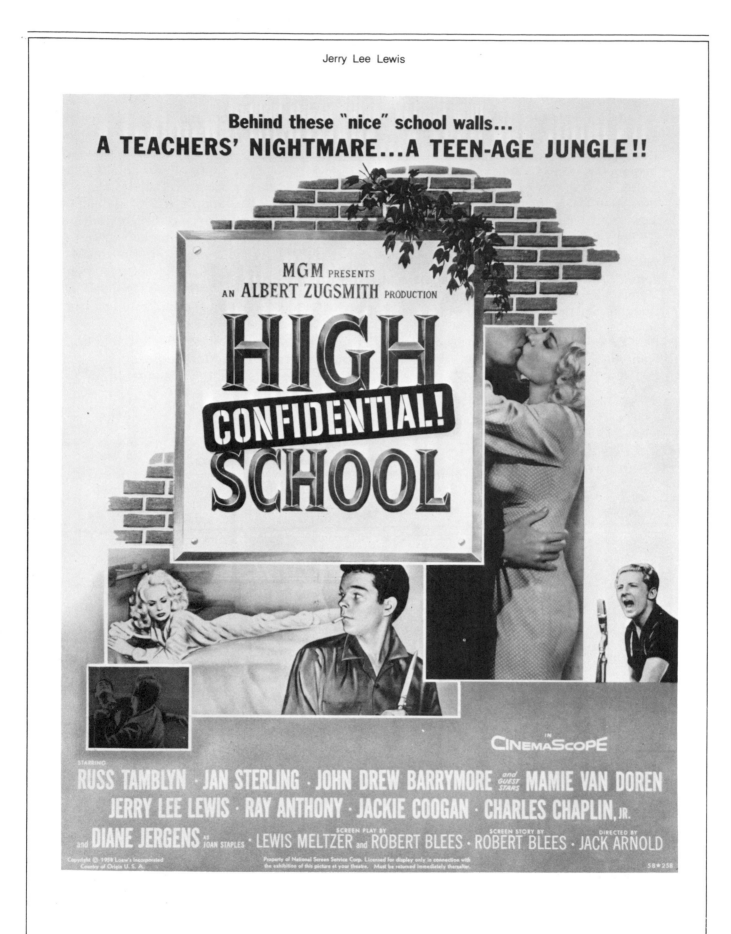

dercover narcotics agent when he registers as a transfer student from Chicago. His brash manner and hipster talk soon ingratiate him with the worst element, and he is on his way to getting the inside track of the ring that supplies "mary jane" (marijuana), pills, and "H" (heroin) to those students hooked or about to be. Tamblyn manages to trap the big wheels in the operation, so the final close-in of other agents nets a big haul in dope and its purveyors.

The screenplay by Lewis Meltzer and Robert Blees, from a story by Blees, is well constructed and faithfully told in the special language of today's juniors. The story seems to have some missing parts, however, nota-

Record sleeve from the gold record "High School Confidential." Left to right: Diane Jergens, Russ Tamblyn, Jan Sterling, John Drew Barrymore, and Mamie Van Doren.

bly the ambiguous relationship of Tamblyn toward Mamie Van Doren, who is described as his "aunt" but who all too obviously has more than substitute maternal feelings for him. Mel Welles has contributed two pieces of special material, one of which, an existentialist poem recited by Phillipa Fallon, is a standout.

Tamblyn, in the role of the narcotics agent masquerading as a problem student, is excellent. Miss Sterling, who must convey both adult maturity as the teacher most involved and yet be convincing as someone to stir the male students to other than scholastic efforts, is most effective. Zugsmith has cast his picture with an array of names—John Drew Barrymore, Jackie Coogan, Charles Chaplin Jr., Jerry Lee Lewis, Mamie Van Doren, and Ray Anthony—as special audience bait. Young Barrymore gives a tough performance, and Coogan does a vivid job as the chief dope peddler. Chaplin is seen too briefly to register. Diane Jergens is attractive as a young victim of the marijuana habit, and others who contribute include Burt Douglas, Michael Landon, Jody Fair, Robin Raymond, James Todd, Lyle Talbot, and William Wellman, Jr.

Jack Arnold's direction is well paced and draws some believable and sharp characterizations. Harold J. Marzorati's photography, art direction by William A. Horning and Hans Peters, sound by Dr. Wesley Miller, and editing by Ben Lewis all contribute to the technically excellent production.

Powr.

Reprinted courtesy of *Variety*

### Be My Guest 1965
### (British)

Competently made second feature with some lively pop moments for younger beat patrons.

London, April 13.

Rank distribution of a Three Kings (Lance Comfort) Production (in association with Harold Shampan and Filmusic). Features David Hemmings, Avril Angers, Joyce Blair, Jerry Lee Lewis, the Nashville Teens, the Zephyrs, Kenny and the Wranglers, Niteshades. Directed by Lance Comfort. Story and screenplay by Lyn Fairhurst; camera, Basil Emmott; editor, Sid Stone; music, Malcolm Lockyer. Reviewed at R.F.D. Theatre, London. Running Time, 82 minutes.

| | |
|---|---|
| Dave | David Hemmings |
| Ricky | Stephen Marriot |
| Phil | John Pike |
| Erica | Andrea Monet |
| Herbert | Ivor Salter |
| Margaret | Diana King |
| Mrs. Pucil | Avril Angers |
| Wanda | Joyce Blair |
| Hilton Bass | David Healey |
| Artie | Tony Wager |
| Routledge | David Lander |
| Matthews | Robin Stewart |
| Dyllis | Monica Evans |
| Stewart | Douglas Ives |

Designed as a second feature pic and to cash in on the still current vogue for the juve pop talent market, this one does its job adequately. Local patrons will enjoy an earful of some of the local groups, but nobody outside the United Kingdom will go overboard. Lyn Fairhurst's script reveals pro know-how, and Lance Comfort is a director with plenty of savvy. Result is an unambitious item that is a cut above many program film fillers.

Slim story line concerns a London family taking over a seaside guest hotel, how it tries to put the guest house on the map, and how the son of the family, with a beat group, gets involved in a talent contest. Latter brings out some conventional double-crossing (tidied up, eventually, by that good old standby, the tape recorder). Situations and dialogue are from hokumsville, but there's plenty of opportunity for a few groups to put over some lively numbers.

Malcolm Lockyer's incidental music is bright and is interpolated by a number of songs of which the title ditty, and "Somebody Help Me," look the likeliest to win honors. The Zephyrs, the Nashville Teens, Kenny and the Wranglers, the Niteshades, and Jerry Lee Lewis all have the chance to do their stuff musically and are okay without starting any new breakthrough in the contemporary music field.

David Hemmings and Andrea Monet put over some calf love romance, somewhat self-consciously with Miss Monet showing her paces as a possible up-and-comer in the soubrette stakes, though a shade short on star sparkle. Ivor Salter and Diana King do their best in Mom and Dad roles, but have little opportunity in conventional situations. Avril Angers, as a battleaxe of a housekeeper, reveals a deft comedy attack.

Miss Angers, an experienced local comedienne, currently playing in "Little Me" in the West End, is inexplicably overlooked in this pix. Other roles that stand out are David Healey, as a genial, egotistic impresario; and, particularly, Joyce Blair, as his girl friend. Miss Blair, though now blonde instead of brunet, has two or three promising spots and proves herself a useful "blonde temptress" type.

Location work in Brighton has the right authenticity and artwork. Sound and lensing are all okay considering that this is a speedily made, inexpensive picture.

Reprinted courtesy of *Variety*          Rich.

### Keep on Rockin'          1972
### Pennebaker Inc.

Producers . . . Richard Burns, George Weiser, Connaught Films Ltd.
Director . . . . . D. A. Pennebaker
Photography . . . Barry Bergthorson, Jim Desmond, Randy Franken, Richard Leiterman, Roger Murphy, Robert Neuwirth, D. A. Pennebaker.
Sound . . . . . . . Wally Heider, Bob Van Dyke, Robert Leacock, Kate Taylor
Running time—95 minutes
No MPAA Rating

"Keep on Rockin' " stars the kings of fifties'

rock 'n' roll, Bo Diddley, Jerry Lee Lewis, Chuck Berry, and Little Richard, as they appeared at the Toronto Rock 'n' Roll Revival.

The film, however, opens in an uncomfortable way—no titles, just disconnected footage of the phantom yin-yang of the sixties, Janis Joplin and Jimi Hendrix. One begins to feel that everything important happened before the film started. One also assumes that D. A. Pennebaker, producer-director-cameraman, intends a documentary explanation of the particular discomfort surrounding the footage of Joplin and Hendrix.

When the titles start running, about six minutes into the action, it appears almost certain that a serious documentary and not just another rock pic is to come. We follow a motorcycle club, cameraman riding double on the choppers, to the stadium where the festival is taking place. The drivers handling the bikes are sharp. The footage can't help but be interesting, as they cut in and out of a limousine motorcade, also on its way to the event.

Once inside the stadium, something goes wrong. One becomes embarrassed by the camera's presence. Much of its movement seems insensitive to the music, especially when there are novel angles and quick cutting. In fact, the camera is about as out of place in its movement as the white, middle-class, northern audience which somehow just can't catch the beat regardless of how enthusiastically they jerk and shimmy.

Of course, it's possible Pennebaker wanted it this way; that he is telling us what a long way it is from Bo Diddley to Mick Jagger. But this seems hardly worth a feature-length film. And besides, if this was the case, why preface the film with the enigmatic appearances of Joplin and Hendrix.

Unfortunately, there appears to be a simpler explanation. Pennebaker entices his audience with promise of a serious documentary, then falls back on the cliches of the rock epics—all in the hope of creating an adult, as well as teen, box office.

Finally, Jimi Hendrix is not Bo Diddley, and the same camera that is part of the Hendrix momentum is sort of a square spectator at the latter's performance. When Chuck Berry sang, "I Drink TNT, I Smoke Dynamite," what we heard and what was seen had little to do with each other.

Paul Vangelisti
Reprinted courtesy of *Hollywood Reporter*

*American Hot Wax*        1978
(Period Musical Drama—Metrocolor)

Paramount Pictures release, produced by Art Linson. Directed by Floyd Mutrux. Screenplay, John Kaye; camera (Metrocolor), William A. Fraker; editors, Danford B. Greene, Melvin Shapiro, Ronald J.

Fagan; music supervision, Kenny Vance; art direction, Elayne Barbara Ceder; set decoration, George Gaines; sound, Robert Knudsen, Thomas Overton; costumes-wardrobe, Robert DeMora, Don Vargas, Mina Mittelman; assistant director, Joe Wallenstein. Reviewed at Paramount Studio, L.A., March 6, 1978. MPAA rating: PG. Running time 91 minutes.

Alan Freed . . . . . . . . . . . . . . . Tim McIntire
Sheryl . . . . . . . . . . . . . . . . . . Fran Drescher
Mookie . . . . . . . . . . . . . . . . . . . . Jay Leno
Teenage Louise . . . . . . . Laraine Newman
The Chesterfields . . . . Carl, Earl Weaver,
Al Chalk, Sam Harkness
Lennie Richfield . . . . . . . . . . . . Jeff Altman
Artie Moress . . . . . . . . . . . . . Moosie Drier
District Attorney . . . . . . . . . . . . John Lehne

*American Hot Wax,* 1978. Clockwise from top left: The Chesterfields, a group formed especially for this film; Jerry Lee; Screamin' Jay Hawkins; the Planotones; Jim McIntyre as Alan Freed; and Chuck Berry.

THE ORIGINAL SOUNDTRACK ALBUM
FROM THE PARAMOUNT MOTION PICTURE
"AMERICAN HOT WAX"

A SPECIALLY-PRICED 2-RECORD SET FEATURING ORIGINAL '50s RECORDINGS BY
CHUCK BERRY, LITTLE RICHARD, JACKIE WILSON, BUDDY HOLLY AND OTHERS, AS WELL AS
LIVE PERFORMANCES FROM THE FILM'S "BROOKLYN PARAMOUNT CONCERT."

Double album from the movie *American Hot Wax* contains live performances of "Great Balls of Fire" and "Whole Lotta Shakin' Goin' On."

Themselves . . . . Chuck Berry, Jerry Lee Lewis, Screamin' Jay Hawkins
Prof. La Plano . . . . . . . . . . . Kenny Vance
Union Man . . . . . . . . . . . . . Elmer Valentine
Record Producer . . . . . . . . Richard Perry

"American Hot Wax" is an unpretentious and enjoyable salute to the Big Beat era of 20–25 years ago when rock 'n' roll was in its infancy. Art Linson's production is pegged around pioneer rock DJ Alan Freed, impersonated quite well by Tim McIntire. Floyd Mutrux directed John Kaye's deliberately skimpy script which allows for a slew of vintage r&r song interpolations. The 91-minute Paramount release is a good commercial bet for the Easter holiday-spring vacation period. Exhibitors should play the film at very high sound volume for maximum audience impact.

The simple conflict in the story centers around efforts by the police to censor rock music. To the authorities, Freed was a Mongol at the city gates; to kids, he was Columbus opening up a new world. Guest appearances by Chuck Berry, Jerry Lee Lewis, and Screamin' Jay Hawkins add verisimilitude to the era portrayed.

Of particular interest is McIntire. The son of John McIntire and Jeanette Nolan, he's a genuine Renaissance man—actor, musician and also busy in trailer voice-overs. The one element recalled from "The Choirboys" is McIntire's memorable performance as a truly despicable cop. In "American Hot Wax" his gruff charisma manifests a warmer and more sympathetic side. He's the latest second-generation performer to arrive—as usual, after a decade or more of hard work—at the brink of broad public and trade recognition.

Production credits are all good. Kenny Vance supervised the strong music production. Rest of featured cast is up to the easy demands of the script: Fran Drescher and Jay Leno as McIntire's aides; Laraine Newman as an aspiring songwriter; Jeff Altman as a hustling record promoter; Moosie Drier as a Buddy Holly groupie; John Lehne as a smut-crusading district attorney.

Freed has often been credited with "inventing" the phrase rock 'n' roll. He didn't. It can be heard in Depression era song lyrics, if not earlier. However, as a popularizer of the phrase in relation to a new music era, he indeed has a secure place in history.

Murf.

Reprinted courtesy of *Variety*

At the Palomino Club, Los Angeles, July 6, 1979.

# At the Palomino

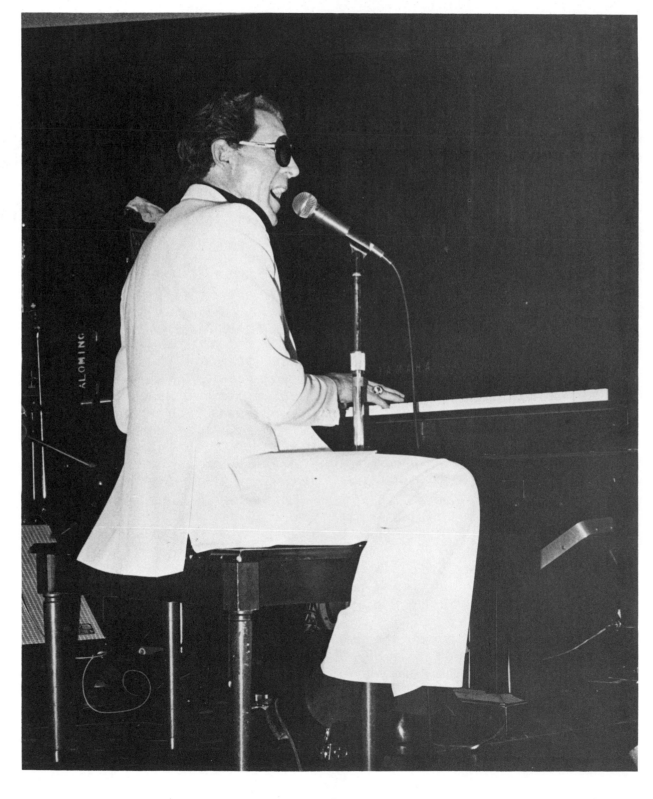

When he goes, there will never
be another Jerry Lee Lewis.
He's one of a kind.

Tommy Thomas

The "Palomino" is America's most honored country and western showcase, having twelve times been awarded by the Country Music Association the title "Number One Country and Western Nightclub." The list of country "superstars" who have appeared there is long: Johnny Cash, Marty Robbins, Willie Nelson, Ray Price, Lynn Anderson, Jerry Lee Lewis, Mickey Gilley, Glen Campbell, Larry Gatlin, Crystal Gayle, Buck Owens, Freddie Hart, Tanya Tucker, Waylon Jennings, Ray Stevens, Rex Allen, etc. In January 1979, Tommy Thomas, owner of the Palomino, described some of his experiences with Jerry Lee Lewis over the years.

*I believe it was 1958—the first time we had Jerry Lee Lewis, it wasn't for much, really, but it was a lot of money in those days, you know. He was one of the superstars that was coming in, and the Palomino invited all of its friends to come down to see the great Jerry Lee Lewis. There were people there from every industry that were really not related to country music. We had the unheard of price of five dollars a ticket at that time. It was in the late fifties when this occurred, and we'd just had Johnny Cash and Marty Robbins and here was Jerry Lee Lewis, another big man, and the Palomino was honored to have such a great man walk into its room. But the people, half the audience, didn't know who he was because they were all promoted to come in the Palomino and buy these five dollar tickets, which was an enormous amount of money in 1958. So he got up and played for all the bankers and the lawyers and doctors and all these big*

*officials—and city fathers. One of the customers came up to me and said, "You know, he's kind of loud." I didn't know Jerry Lee Lewis then, so I went up to him and said, "Hey, Jerry, could you play it down a little bit?" He turned it up louder. Man, I thought, he's loud and people are complaining, so I thought maybe he didn't hear me. So, I went back to him again and said, "Hey, it's kind of loud—could you turn it down a little bit." From then on he went wild; he turned that sound system on as loud as it could go and he kicked the living hell out of that piano. When it was all over with, the piano was in pieces! I learned, you know, you don't go and tell Jerry Lee Lewis how to play the piano. He could care less about my opinion, and I told my friends, "You see what you got me into." I said, "You really got me in trouble now."*

We always have an exciting show at the Palomino, and all the artists do well here.

*I've heard from other sources that they had problems with Jerry. I could never imagine why because he was always way ahead of schedule, and he goes by your word. If you promise him something, you better deliver. Now it's many years later and he's in a five thousand a day class. That's a lot of money for a nightclub—we'll charge the ultimate. Now, Jerry Lee Lewis is coming in for two days. It's been some time now—oh, maybe it's been eight or ten years—since he worked here last. And there are conditions: he's got to have a limousine; he's got to have a suite for himself; he's got to have a baby grand in his suite; and he's got to have*

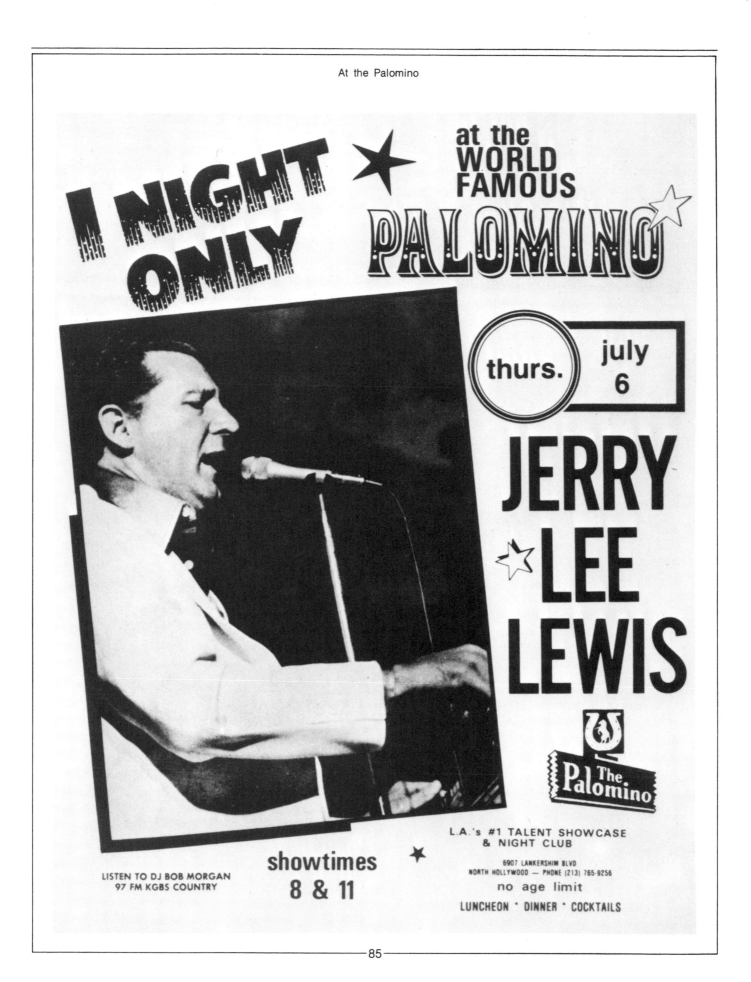

Left to right: J. W. Whitten, JLL's road manager; Tommy Thomas, owner of the Palomino Club; and Jerry Lee.

With Linda Gail Lewis, January 1968, at the Palomino.

With Dottie West.

With Ron Wood of the Rolling Stones.

Dick Clark and "The Killer."

With John Belushi.

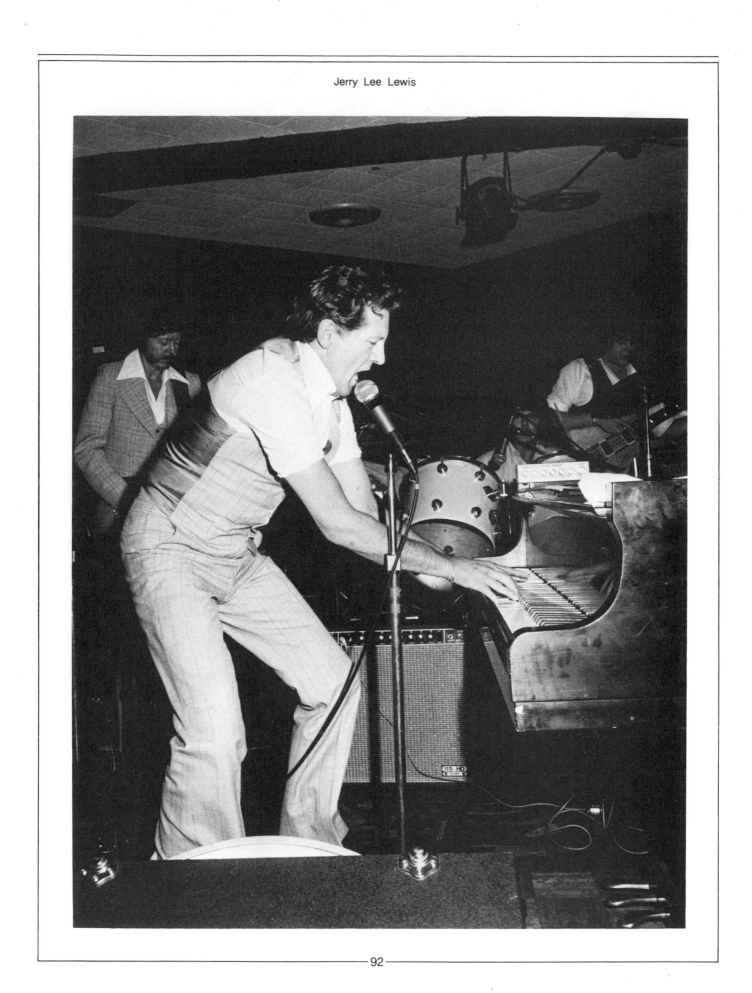

rooms for his band—six more rooms! So we said, "That's no problem, we'll take care of it," and we went to Howard Johnson's and made all the arrangements with the day manager. Every week we call up, and they tell us, "Don't worry, don't worry, don't worry," so along comes Jerry Lee Lewis, and the day manager doesn't tell the night manager and gives away his suite!

Jerry Lee Lewis calls and says, "I'm going to cancel the date—I have no place to stay," and I can't believe it! I'm panicking. It cost me plenty—I had to go and buy out the guy who had the suite and get him another room in another hotel or I'd lose the act! It could have been a disaster. . . .

But he's a "legend." How many people are around now that started like he did with Elvis Presley and Johnny Cash and all those people. . . .

Jerry Lee Lewis is one of the originals, there's only one Jerry Lee Lewis—he came from that era. There are only a few of those people left: they are the ones that started rock 'n' roll. They were way ahead of everybody. They went through all the years of criticism: the ups and downs. Their music has always been recognized by people all over the world. When they sing or entertain, they entertain for the world: everybody loves them. Certain artists just entertain for a small group of people—they specialize in one type of music. Jerry Lee Lewis is a world famous artist: he's not just national. Reviewers and music critics recognize this fact. After Elvis Presley passed away, the critics realized that there were only a few of those people left that started all of this.

Jerry Lee Lewis's biggest fans happen to be men very heavily into the music business—like music critics . . . rock critics . . . fellow musicians . . . record industry people. He brings in the heavy spenders: businessmen. People who are his age who started out years ago with nothing and who have become successful in business or industry. You know, I never thought of it that way before, but he does have a very macho image about him.

When he goes . . . that's the end of an era. He is a specialist, just like Jimmy Durante was a specialist in his field. Like Elvis, like any great artist who started a certain trend: when he goes, there will never be another Jerry Lee Lewis.

As Iago in *Catch My Soul.*

# 9
# Catch My Soul

In March of 1968 Jerry's career took a new direction: He tackled the starring role in a musical adaptation of Shakespeare's *Othello* called *Catch My Soul.* The play was the brainchild of Jack Good, pioneer of rock 'n' roll on British Television and creator of the highly successful American TV production *Shindig.* This play, which ran for six weeks at the Ahmanson Theatre in Los Angeles, was one of the first efforts to blend rock 'n' roll music with legitimate theater. *Catch My Soul* was financially successful even though the play received mixed reviews.

(Following review courtesy *Los Angeles Times*)

### Jerry Lee Lewis in 'Soul' Puts Shakespeare on Rocks

#### by Pete Johnson

The words are Shakespeare's, the speech Iago's in "Othello," its reference to the fading fortune of Michael Cassio, damned by a drunken quarrel set up by the conniving Iago. But the philosophy also applies to the conniver, within the context of the play and without.

Jerry Lee Lewis, a 31-year-old Louisiana boy last seen in the role of Jerry Lee Lewis, the bemopped piano destroyer who sang such hits as "Whole Lotta Shakin' Goin' On," "Great Balls of Fire," "Breathless" and "High School Confidential," is the newest heir to the role of Iago, a part he will play in a rocking version of "Othello" (retitled "Catch My Soul") which opens Tuesday in the Ahmanson Theatre of the Music Center.

Iago's thoughts on reputations have a pointed irony when drawled softly from the mouth of Lewis. His reputation and career were crippled in the summer of 1958 when he married his 13-year-old cousin Myra ("She was actually 14," he says now, "but all the news reports had her as 13").

The marriage was announced as "High School Confidential" was climbing the charts, helped by its tie-in with the movie of the same name. Suddenly you could not hear the record on any station—incensed program directors pulled it from their play lists and refused to air subsequent records by the singer, who had been on a hot streak of hits. His performances prompted demonstrations, and he had trouble with English authorities during a foreign tour.

Ten years later, still married to Myra, now 23 with a 4-year-old daughter, Phoebe, Lewis is again respectable, making a good living from performances and records, directed primarily at the country and western field which spawned him. His last memorable hit was a thumping version of "High Heel Sneakers" a couple of years ago but his name is still powerful enough to assure him a comfortable livelihood.

"Who steals my purse steals trash," spouts Iago. " 'Tis something, nothing; 'twas mine, 'tis his, and has been slave to thousands; but he who filches from me my good name robs me of that which not enriches him and makes me poor indeed."

So this good rock-roots name, touring the country in a robust limousine, was offered a Shakespearean role and, after a little thought, decided to take it.

"I didn't know much about Shakespeare

Iago with Othello, right, played by William Marshall.

before this," he says. "I hadn't studied it or read at it. I was very surprised. Jack Good (who conceived and is directing the current production) told me about it when we did the last 'Shindig' show."

Good, who produced the television series, had been thinking of a rock version of "Othello" for about 10 years. He began seriously working on it in 1962, writing a modern dialect script which he subsequently scrapped.

Three years ago, he says, "I had the spine of it down and most of the lyrics set. I started bullying Ray Pohlman to write the music." The working version leaves Shakespeare little changed, other than modernizing *thee*'s and *thou*'s and obscure references. "In this play," explains Good, "Iago is a Machiavellian stage manager. Jerry's piano becomes an infernal instrument for his soliloquies to the audience. It is a console of evil.

"Thus the band and the piano become an integral part of the play, and Jerry's speeches become the performance of a blues singer speaking to the people."

Good says that Lewis was one of the first people he had in mind for the play. "I feel very glad to have this bugger because he's really himself, he's not trying to be anything else. When he's going, everything he says is smash down the middle true. Down-home country truth. It's like his records; it's him.

He doesn't recognize any laws or rules: he just makes it fit for him. He sort of makes the lines his own."

Lewis learned his part by reading the play into a tape recorder, minus the lines of Iago, and running the tape as he toured in his Lincoln limousine last year until he could spout all of Iago's speeches.

"Iago really puts out some words in this thing [the singer remarks]. I never knew there was so many words. Shakespeare . . . [he shakes his head slowly] was really something. [He brightens slyly.] I wonder what he would of thought of my records?

"This is the first acting I've ever done. I like it. I'd really like to get into it all the way. I'll never give up music—it's my life—but with a little experience I might be an actor. I am surrounded by some real great actors, and that's wonderful, and it kind of makes me look good, too.

"I think the generation today who don't know much about stage plays will come here and enjoy it. They'd be out of their minds if they didn't. It has everything: rhythm and blues, rock 'n' roll, country and western, serious acting, comedy, drama. Everything."

Watching a rehearsal, it takes a couple of moments to reconcile memories of the fluorescent blond wildman whose hairdo streamed across his face as he vanquished the piano in a two-fisted battle to the soft-spoken drawling actor, now a brunet with a thin mustache trickling down both sides of his chin.

His hair looks a bit shorter, but he promises to have it dyed back into prominence for the performance. Lewis's accent unglues some of the formality of Elizabethan sentence structure without disturbing the force of his speeches.

He is enthusiastic about his singing numbers, which were written for him. "My four songs are so good, I'd like to cut some records with them. I think it could do me a lot of good."

Lewis lives on Coro Lake, near Memphis, but has temporarily relocated his family in Los Angeles for the six-week production.

His only complaint about the new venture is the food in Los Angeles, which he finds inferior to his customary Southern fare, so he rarely ventures away from his wife's kitchen for meals.

Others in the cast of "Catch My Soul" (the title comes from one of Othello's lines, "Perdition, catch my soul, but I do love thee") are William Marshall, Julienne Marie, Gerianne Raphael, William Jordan, Gloria Jones, William Lanteau, Wesdon Bishop, and Joseph Mascolo.

Lewis's frenetic piano playing (he expects to go through two or three instruments during the six weeks) will be augmented by a 17-piece band of predominantly rock structure; two guitars, three percussionists, bass, organ, two drums, seven-piece brass section and (oddly) a harp.

The conjunction of Jerry Lee Lewis and William Shakespeare appears to corrupt neither side. Iago becomes Lewis as much as Lewis becomes Iago because, as Good explains, "Jerry is not on a voyage of discovery. He is one of those persons who exists like the fixed points of the compass by which everything else must be judged. Thirty-one years of southern individuality is not about to be bent out of shape by 364 years of dramatic tradition."

## THE CAST
### In Order of Appearance

| | |
|---|---|
| Iago | Jerry Lee Lewis |
| Othello | William Marshall |
| Desdemona | Julienne Marie |
| Cassio | William Jordan |
| Emilia | Gerrianne Raphael |
| Roderigo | William Lanteau |
| Montano | Wesdon Bishop |
| Bianca | Gloria Jones |
| Lodovico | Joseph Mascolo |
| Sax Man | Dick Caruso |

## PRINCIPALS

WILLIAM MARSHALL, Othello, born and reared in Gary, Indiana, was invited by Gate Theatre Productions to play Othello in the 1962 Dublin Theatre Festival, in which he was hailed, and subsequently [he] toured Switzerland, Luxembourg, Belgium, and the Netherlands. His first stage appearance had been in *Carmen Jones,* and he had served as proxy for Boris Karloff in the role of Captain Hook in *Peter Pan.* He appeared in *Lost in the Stars,* in *The Green Pastures* as God, and in *Oedipus Rex, The Emperor Jones,* and *Toys in the Attic.* He has been seen in films such as *Lydia Bailey, Demetrius and the Gladiators, Something of Value,* and *Sabu and the Magic Ring*; and has been guest star on many prominent TV series. His pilot show for *The Man from U.N.C.L.E.* was released as a feature film entitled *To Trap a Spy.*

JERRY LEE LEWIS, Iago, is the boy from Louisiana who set America rocking on its heels when he launched his swinging, wild, fun-loving sound early in 1958. Jerry created his own style of music by improvisation, incorporating the boogie and the blues of the South with country music, exploding one musical idea after another. This resulted in

With Jack Good, director of "Catch My Soul."

such million-record sellers as "Great Balls of Fire," "Breathless," "Whole Lot of Shakin'," and "High School Confidential." Jerry was born in Ferriday, Louisiana. His youthful ambition to become a preacher changed to a musical career which began with playing drums at the Wagon Wheel in Natchez, Mississippi. Never having taken a formal music lesson in his life, a self-taught musician on fiddle, drums, and piano, Jerry played with trios, orchestras, and other combos until finally he was signed to a recording contract in 1956. Jerry now makes his home on Coro Lake, near Memphis, Tennessee.

WILLIAM JORDAN, Cassio, recently contracted for five motion pictures by producer-director Sergio Leone, made his professional bow in 1965 in the touring company of *Who's Afraid of Virginia Woolf?* with Shelley Winters. Critical acclaim led to *The Lion in Winter* with George C. Scott and Colleen Dewhurst and *The Glass Menagerie* with Elizabeth Hartman and Mercedes McCambridge. In 1966, he made his first Broadway appearance in *Wait Until Dark.* This past year, Mr. Jordan commuted between New York and Hollywood television assignments, calling home his 40-acre farm in Connecticut.

THE BLOSSOMS: Darlene Love, Fanita James, and Jean King joined voices eight years ago to sing at school functions. Since then they have progressed through groups called Richard Berry and the Dreamers, The Bobb B. Sox, and the Blue Jeans and their hit record "Zippadidoda," until at last they emerged as themselves: the Blossoms. They toured leading supper clubs with the Righteous Brothers, and have backed every major recording artist in the business. By virtue of their long and successful tenure with *Shindig,* the Blossoms probably had more television exposure than any other singing group. They also sang the motion picture themes for *John Goldfarb, Move Over Darling, Beach Blanket Bingo,* and Henry Mancini's title tune for the soon to be released *The Party.*

JACK GOOD, director, was born in London and graduated with a degree in philology from Balliol College, Oxford, where he was president of the Oxford University Dramatic Society. He studied acting at the London Academy of Music and Art and the Poetry Society of London, Toynbee Hall. He acted in London's West End, on Broadway in *The Affair,* in motion pictures which included *Father Goose* with Cary Grant, and directed a substantial number of stage classics from the Greek and Shakespeare canons. Mr. Good pioneered in the rhythm and blues vogue producing the first album in England, and subsequently ABC-TV's *Shindig* in the U.S. and the first special for the Beatles, "Around the Beatles." This past season he conceived and supervised the NBC special "Love, Andy," starring Andy Williams.

RAY POHLMAN, composer, a highly versatile music man, is in top demand, whether for feature films, television, or recordings. During his early years in the music industry, he toured with dance bands and musical groups and was a featured singer with Kay Starr for three years in leading supper clubs throughout the nation. He was musical director for ABC's *Shindig,* the first nationally telecast show of its kind. Mr. Pohlman is the recipient of three Gold Records and a Gold Album for his arrangements for leading recording artists and groups.

RAY AGHAYAN, costume designer, has created costumes for such stars as Judy Garland, Andy Williams, Doris Day, Dean Martin, Barbra Streisand, Fred Astaire, and Dinah Shore, and designed over 300 television shows for NBC including "The Julie Andrews Special," "Carol Channing and 101 Men," "The Danny Thomas Specials," and the new musical version of Robin Hood. 1967 proved to be his prize year in which, sharing credit with Bob Mackie for the television special, "Alice Through The Looking Glass," he won an Emmy Award for costume design, the first such award in television history; the Costume Designers' Guild Award

for the same show; and the French Prestige Award for his work on the motion picture, *Doctor Dolittle,* another "first" to a designer in film. Other motion pictures which he has designed are *Caprice, In Like Flint, Glass Bottom Boat, Our Man Flint, Do Not Disturb,* and *The Art of Love.*

# 10

# Sun Records Today:
## An Interview with Shelby Singleton

> Presley was always just amazed
> and intrigued by Jerry Lee's
> unique piano style.
>
> Shelby Singleton

**S**helby Singleton has been referred to as one of the shrewdest businessmen on the country music scene. In the music field he's done it all: a promotion man, product manager, record producer, record company owner, and head of his own publishing firm—these are just some of the titles he's had in his long and successful career. In his nine years with Mercury Records he rose to the position of vice-president of A & R (Artist and Repertoire) and was responsible for bringing Jerry Lee Lewis and Charlie Rich to Smash Records (a division of Mercury). In 1966 he resigned his position at Mercury to form his own label, Plantation Records. He purchased Sun Records in the late sixties. The following interview was taped on February 3, 1979, at the Sun offices.

**Robert Cain:**
When did you first take over Sun Records?

**Shelby Singleton, Jr.:**
Actually, I bought Sun Records as of July 1, 1969.

**Cain:**
Did you have any idea at that time that the interest in old records would be as great as it turned out to be?

**Singleton:**
Well, I had an intuition, or whatever you want to call it, that the catalog of Sun, which contained what I thought were some of the most valuable recording artists that had ever been recorded in a small catalog, would become important basically because of Johnny Cash more than any other act at that time. However, we have hundreds of sides of Jerry Lee Lewis, quite a few by Roy Orbison, and a ton by Charlie Rich and other acts that became more important as time went on. At that particular time, we bought the catalog basically on what we knew we could do with the Johnny Cash product since Johnny Cash that summer was starting a summer replacement television show.

**Cain:**
Were you surprised when Jerry Lee Lewis seemed to be your best seller?

**Singleton:**
No. Having a past history with Jerry Lee, we knew that he is subject to explode at any time, and the scope of his recording has really broadened throughout the years. During his fifteen years with Mercury, he bridged the gap from rock 'n' roll to country very successfully. And by doing this, he did not lose any rock audience—which some acts do whenever they change directions or go from one type of music to another.

**Cain:**
What's he like in the recording studio?

**Singleton:**
He is, in a recording studio, very similar to what he is onstage. Very unpredictable. I've seen the times you could go into the recording studio with Jerry Lee and cut maybe six or seven songs in a three-hour period. I've seen other times that you could go in and you couldn't get one good one. A lot of times

this would be because Jerry Lee didn't like the particular songs that he was doing, I'm sure. Again, maybe the musicians weren't clicking with what he was doing. So there's all kinds of reasons involved in it. Basically, he is unique in the fact that he does not have to study a song very long to sing it. He can hear a song once or twice, and he'll play it and sing it. . . . I mean, it's not what we would call a manufactured talent, it's more of a natural talent.

**Cain:**
I've heard from some people that he often prides himself on the ability to cut a record in one take.

**Singleton:**
Well, I would say that that is true on the majority of his recordings, but it just depends on the particular song. If it's a song he likes, and the arrangement is together on the first take and you don't have to change the music, usually Jerry Lee's part is right.

**Cain:**
What is the reaction internationally (in England, Holland) to Sun Records in general and Jerry Lee specifically?

**Singleton:**
Well, according to our licensees in these territories, Sun Records is probably the best-known American record label, and there is a gigantic movement of collectors and fans of Sun Records and the Sun sound basically in England, Holland, Germany, and Scandinavia more than anyplace else. Quite a few in Australia, but. . . . Jerry Lee has an international fan club, an organization which he personally . . . probably . . . has nothing to do with. He has his fans, who put out magazines, who do publicity, who follow everything that Jerry Lee does, whether it's in the United States or it's in England, or whether it's in Germany or France, or whatever it may be. With this type of fol-

lowing, anything new that comes out —especially if it is rock or rockabilly—is automatically released in these territories and has a built-in sales potential. I would say that this is not true with Jerry Lee's real straight country stuff, but it is true of his rock and rockabilly stuff.

**Cain:**
If you take the list of the artists on the Sun roster such as Elvis Presley, Johnny Cash, Charlie Rich, Roy Orbison, Carl Perkins, etc., you could probably draw a circle on the map of the United States and maybe in a hundred- or two-hundred-square-mile area cover where almost all of these people have come from. Can you figure why so many incredibly talented people all seem to have come from essentially the same area?

**Singleton:**
Well, there are probably more talented people walking the streets today that have never been exposed to the public than there are ones that are making phonograph records, and there's a lot of reasons for that. The basic reason is that, first of all, the people who had the know-how and the technical knowledge to make the phonograph records made them unique. Secondly, the ability to select from the talent that you mentioned probably five or six entirely unique voices and styles. So the fact that these acts came through Memphis and the Sun Studios really does not mean that the same type of thing could not happen someplace else.

**Cain:**
Approximately how many sides do you think you have in your Sun Library of Jerry Lee?

**Singleton:**
I really don't know. Every time we started going through tapes, we have found sides with Jerry Lee singing on them that we didn't know existed. I'd say in the neighborhood of four to five hundred different sides.

**Cain:**
Since Jerry Lee has recently signed with Electra, do you feel that the release of records by Jerry on Electra will dissipate sales on your Sun label, or will actually give them a lift?

**Singleton:**
Well, it depends on what kind of music they cut. If they're successful in continuing Jerry Lee's string of hits, of course it always helps our sales. It does hurt, however, if they start driving nails in his coffin (as I call it, for every time they come out with a record that doesn't hit), they will muddy up the water, more or less, and what we're hoping is that they will go after Jerry Lee in the pop and rock and underground market and leave the country market alone with him and try to re-establish him as a rock star. If they do—and they really have the ability from their sales and merchandising division to do this type of thing—of course it will make our catalog that much stronger.

**Cain:**
During the careers of Elvis Presley and Jerry Lee Lewis, I imagine they were competitors. Were they friends out of the recording studio, or were they competitors socially?

**Singleton:**
There are very few artists that ever become friends with another artist. It's really by nature of the fact that people go in different ways . . . if they're really successful in what they're doing. I would say that—from the stories that we hear, and the people that are involved—that Presley was always just amazed and intrigued by Jerry Lee's unique piano style and Presley wanted to be a piano player. And, of course, he was not. (He was not a very good musician of any type as far as a musical instrument was concerned.) He was very much intrigued by Jerry Lee's piano playing where, on the other hand, I think Jerry Lee was intrigued

by the idol worship that people had for Presley. And, in the beginning, I would say that they were casual friends. I don't think that they were ever competitors because they were never really on the same level. As Presley was always very secluded and very protected—very manageable; Jerry Lee was entirely the opposite. He was always very open and very flashy. He'd go into a town and he'd want everybody to know he was there: he didn't take a back seat to anybody . . . very outspoken and not apologetic for anything. You'd just have to say that they were casual friends in the beginning and worked together and then, as time went on, they both went their own way and made their own niche in different fields.

**Cain:**
Would you say that the style of Jerry Lee's piano is something he developed on his own, or was he influenced by any particular entertainer?

**Singleton:**
The style is very reminiscent of what Moon Mulligan used to do. . . . I would say there's an influence of country and blues piano that probably came from the fact that Jerry Lee listened to New Orleans music from Ferriday, and that's how that style was developed. Plus, it has a touch of gospel in it, and, of course, with his cousin Jimmy Swaggart, who's a gospel preacher, and cousin Mickey Gilley, who is an entertainer, their styles are exactly the same. Whether they just happened to develop this as an in-born talent is really unknown. It could be a style that came from that particular location in the country.

**Cain:**
I have heard that a recording session with Jerry Lee often ends up as a family reunion with aunts, uncles, and cousins showing up. Is that true?

**Singleton:**
That happens a lot of times.

**Cain:**
Is it disturbing?

**Singleton:**
Well, to some people it may be. It depends on the producer's power of concentration. The only thing we ever objected to when we were recording with Jerry Lee was when all the kids showed up, and they would run up and down the control room screaming and shouting while he was trying to make a recording. Actually, the opinions of the kinfolks are just as important as the opinions of the public. Usually it was a pretty good test of what they liked or what they didn't like because they knew just about as much about Jerry Lee as anybody.

**Cain:**
Part of the unique "Sun sound" was an echo effect or flutter echo effect. Could you explain what that is?

**Singleton:**
That is what was known in those days as "tape echo," and it was done by taking one tape and playing it and running another tape at the same time, and patching the two together so that the second one ran at a little bit slower speed to get an echo effect. In other words, there were two tapes actually duplicating one another at different speeds that made the echo sound. That is what we refer to today as tape echo. There are many different kinds of echoes. There is chamber echo; there is electric echo. There is some equipment made in Germany that goes into a steel pin that captures the sound, and you

can adjust it to any kind of echo that you want. But this particular echo system did not echo just individual instruments or individual voices, it actually echoed the whole track, and that is where that effect came from.

**Cain:**
Many people believe that, had Jerry Lee been managed by Colonel Parker, he would have become a much greater star. What is your opinion?

**Singleton:**
Well, I agree with that. I think Jerry Lee Lewis is a success in spite of himself. It is hard for him to take direction. It is very hard for anybody to say, "Here, Jerry Lee: This is what you are going to do," and for him to follow through with it. I think he is a very headstrong person and has his own opinions about what he should do or shouldn't do.

**Cain:**
Did you ever meet Jerry Lee's father, Elmo?

**Singleton:**
Yes, I did meet Elmo. Elmo, in my opinion, was a very nice—what we call down-to-earth—country person. He was awed by his son's success. He spent many hours of labor when Jerry Lee was growing up, working on the farm, working from daylight to dark to get his family something. When Jerry Lee finally did make it as an artist, Jerry Lee was a very protective person as far as his family were concerned and was very close to his mother and his father, and also his sisters. He just loves his family, as most people who were raised in the country do.

**Cain:**
You have presented Jerry Lee with several gold singles.

**Singleton:**
Yes, eight or ten.

**Cain:**
Was there any inscription on these records?

**Singleton:**
Yes, they read: TO JERRY LEE LEWIS, WORLD'S GREATEST ENTERTAINER!

**Cain:**
Well, I guess that says it all.

# 11

# Tom Jones and the "Killer":
## An Interview

As far as contemporary
music from the fifties on,
Jerry Lee Lewis has been
my biggest influence.
I've bought more records of
Jerry Lee Lewis than any other
entertainer.

Tom Jones

**E**ver since his first million-seller record, "It's Not Unusual," propelled him to stardom in 1965, Tom Jones has been the object of critical acclaim around the world. Many have hailed him as the Welsh Elvis Presley. This dynamic performer has thrilled audiences from South Africa to New York, from Hollywood to Texas, and Alabama to Canada. Truly an international favorite, he is the proud possessor of nine Gold Records, which include: "It's Not Unusual," "Green Green Grass of Home," "What's New, Pussycat," "Delilah," and "She's a Lady." Tom Jones may be best known in America for his highly successful television show *This Is Tom Jones,* which ran for three years. The relationship between Tom and Jerry Lee began typically as that of a young fan for an established star. Over the years this changed to a feeling of mutual admiration from one star to another. The following interview was taped during Tom Jones's engagement at Caesars Palace in Las Vegas, April 1980.

**Robert Cain:**
I was told by Gary Scala, the former president of the Jerry Lee Lewis Fan Club, that you were once a member. Is that true?

**Tom Jones:**
That is true.

**Cain:**
And about when was that?

**Jones:**
In, let me see, that was the early sixties, about maybe 1960, '61.

**Cain:**
Is there any particular reason why you focused on Jerry Lee Lewis?

**Jones:**
Yes, I think the first thing that struck me was his vocal ability. I think when rock 'n' roll was big in the late fifties and early sixties, Jerry Lee was the best singer, you know—had the best voice.

**Cain:**
When did you first meet Jerry Lee in person?

**Jones:**
I met Jerry Lee in the early sixties. I think it was about 1963.

I saw him in a club in London. That's when I first met him—the first time I ever saw him was in Cardiff, in South Wales (which was in '57 when he first came over)—but I met him outside a club in London. I'd just moved to London myself, and I was trying to get a record contract. You know, it was just sort of shaking hands, and I told him I was a big fan of his and I was trying to get a record released at the time.

**Cain:**

In 1968 Jerry Lee switched from rock 'n' roll to the country field, and many of his fans were upset at this. What was your reaction to this switch?

**Jones:**

Well, to me it wasn't really a switch because Jerry Lee had always sung country songs on a lot of B sides of his rock 'n' roll singles. I noticed that there would be a country song on the flip side. So it's just that he leaned more toward country music than to rock 'n' roll. I don't think it was a complete switch. It was just that he did more country than he did rock.

**Cain:**

I was told by Shelby Singleton in Nashville that there is an amazing interest in England in Sun Records and Jerry Lee Lewis.

**Jones:**

Yes, with English people, especially people that are interested in rock 'n' roll. You know, when I used to collect rock 'n' roll records in the fifties and in the sixties, we always wanted to know where the record was made and who produced it, who was on lead guitar, who was on drums. People that were interested in rock 'n' roll wanted to know exactly who was making the record apart from who was the star. They wanted to know everybody else that was on the record. Everybody knew that Jerry Lee recorded on Sun Records, and they knew that Sam Phillips was his producer at that time and who the drummer was, who the guitarist was, so Sun Records became famous because of the people that were recording for the record label.

The same goes for . . . well, like when James Burton started playing guitar for Elvis Presley. People knew who James Burton

was in England because he played lead guitar for Ricky Nelson. He was surprised when he went over to England thinking that he would only be known for playing guitar for Elvis. A lot of people knew who he was because he played guitar for Ricky Nelson, but he wasn't aware that people knew that.

**Cain:**

I have heard from reliable sources there is a very interesting story behind your hit record, "The Green Green Grass of Home," that involves Jerry Lee Lewis. Is that true?

**Jones:**

That is true. The first time I heard "The Green Green Grass of Home" was on a Jerry Lee album which was called *Country Songs for City Folks,* and I bought it in New York in '67. I think it was either 1966 or '67. I went into one of the record shops in New York and said, "Do you have Jerry Lee Lewis's latest album?" And it was *Country Songs for City Folks.* I listened to the album, and "The Green Green Grass of Home" stood out in the album. So when I went back to England I said to my manager, "You know there's this great song on the Jerry Lee Lewis album. I would like to give it a try." So I recorded it and that's when it became a hit, and that's where I found it. If I hadn't bought that album, I might never have heard the song.

**Cain:**

On March 28, 1969, Jerry Lee Lewis appeared on your television show. The expression on your face while you were watching him would be hard to describe. Can you recall at all your feelings at that moment?

**Jones:**

The reason why it felt so good is because since I have been collecting Jerry Lee Lewis records, I have been singing myself. I have always been singing all my life. I used to sing in small clubs in South Wales with a small group that I had. We did a lot of Jerry

Lee Lewis songs. People knew that I dug Jerry Lee more than any other rock 'n' roll singer, and I said, "One day I will work with this man. I am sure that I'll be on the same stage as him and that I'll work with him. I'll do a duet with him in some way." You know, when I had him on my own show, it was a great thrill. I was actually watching him performing. It was like a dream come true.

**Cain:**
Between the rock 'n' roll field and the country field, Jerry has had some thirty-five or forty hits. Are there any of those which are particular favorites of yours?

**Jones:**
Yes, I think as far as the rock 'n' roll records are concerned. The first one, of course, is "A Whole Lot of Shakin' Goin' On" because that was the first song I ever heard him sing, so that would be one of my favorites. I think the best rock 'n' roll record he ever made was "Great Balls of Fire." The original recording of that is a rock 'n' roll classic. It's so perfect there's not one thing wrong with it. You couldn't better it in any way. I would think that as far as contemporary music from the fifties on, Jerry Lee Lewis has been my biggest influence. I've bought more records of Jerry Lee Lewis than any other entertainer. Every record he's ever made anyway.

**Cain:**
You and me both. Many people refer to Jerry Lee Lewis as a living legend. Would you agree with that statement?

**Jones:**
Yes, I believe that Jerry Lewis is one of the originators of rock 'n' roll. I think his style is unique anyway. His interpretation of rock 'n' roll is different from anybody else's. So, therefore, I think he's unique. He's still doing it today. He does the same today as he did when he started. He can still do it. So you know he is a living legend. If he were dead,

they would call him a legend. So thank God, he's still alive, so he's a living legend.

**Cain:**
Outside of the television show that you two did together, have you ever appeared on-stage in Las Vegas or anywhere else together?

**Jones:**
No, the only time that we've ever sung together was in my dressing room. He came over to see me—let me see, I think it was two years ago now. He came into the dressing room, and we sang together. We have a piano in the dressing room and we ran through a bunch of stuff that he'd recorded. He forgot the words, and I remembered them. When you listen to someone's records and you like them so much, you remember the words more than they do because if somebody wanted me to sing a lot of songs that I've recorded, I wouldn't remember the words, but if they liked a particular song, they would.

**Cain:**
I have spoken to many people about Jerry Lee Lewis—disc jockeys, club owners, record company owners. Most of them agree: they call him the most honest person you would ever want to meet. Do you agree with that?

**Jones:**
Yes, I think he knows what he wants to do and he does it. He's always been dedicated to the music that he likes to do, and that's what he does. He is Jerry Lee Lewis. If you wanted him to do something else, then you better call in another performer. I mean he does what he does and he admits that.

**Cain:**
Numerous people in the music business have stated that had Jerry Lee Lewis had the benefit of the genius of Colonel Tom Parker,

he would have been an even greater star. Do you agree?

**Jones:**
Well, I think that the difference between Elvis Presley and Jerry Lee is that Elvis realized that he needed guidance. That's why he went to Colonel Tom Parker. I think he realized he had to have a manager and to listen to him. It would be more difficult to manage Jerry Lee. He knows what he wants himself. . . . I think he is his own man.

**Cain:**
You mean he's more opinionated?

**Jones:**
Yes, he's more opinionated. It would be more difficult for him to listen to somebody else. I've talked to him about that myself. His views on managers are not very—well, he doesn't think too much of them. That could have come up from bad management. A rough deal in the beginning. But I'm sure that if he could have been handled like Elvis Presley, if it was at all possible, he would be a much bigger star.

**Cain:**
If there were such a thing as a rock 'n' roll hall of fame, where would you rank Jerry Lee Lewis in that place?

**Jones:**
Well, for my own personal taste I would think that he would be Number One.

# The Country Years:

## An Interview with Jerry Kennedy

> "... I guess that old piano
> is my best friend and the stage
> is my home. So if I don't stay
> on top I got nowhere to go."

Jerry Lee Lewis

In 1968 Jerry's career took a major turn. Since signing with Smash Records in '63, Jerry and his record producers had tried with limited success to reactivate public interest in him as a rock 'n' roll performer.

During the period between '63 and '68 several good rock records were released by the Killer and his producer, Shelby Singleton. The first was *The Golden Hits of Jerry Lee Lewis,* which was a compilation of most of his best-selling singles from the early days on Sun. A valiant attempt, but sales did not live up to expectations.

Next came *The Greatest Live Show on Earth,* a superb album with the sounds and excitement of fifteen thousand shouting Alabamians at the Birmingham Municipal Auditorium, cheering Jerry on—he never sounded better. Although this album is no longer in print it has become a rock classic and is sought by collectors. The single "High Heel Sneakers" came from this album and received a great deal of air play, which is notable because in many areas the ban on his records was still in effect. Mercury released several live records after this but none of them completely captured the fire and intense enthusiasm of this amazing album. It was followed by *The Return of Rock.* A good album, but once again sales were disappointing.

Jerry's records were selling, but not setting the charts on fire. Disc jockeys were airing his disks, but not frequently. The task of returning Jerry Lee Lewis to the top ten was proving more difficult than had been expected. Then something happened which made a difficult task almost impossible: THE BRITISH INVASION!

In January 1964 Capitol Records released a recording by a new English group called the Beatles. The single, "I Want to Hold Your Hand," was backed by a massive publicity campaign informing America that "The Beatles Are Coming." When they finally arrived in the U.S. in February, they were greeted at the airport by over ten thousand screaming fans. Beatlemania had begun. Overnight Beatle haircuts were the rage. Solo artists who were a hot property in the fifties were out; group mania was in. The Beatles were followed in quick succession by the Rolling Stones, the Animals, the Kinks, the Dave Clark Five, the Zombies, Them, Herman's Hermits, Gerry and the Pacemakers, etc. Almost every passing month saw the emergence of yet another English group with a top ten record. These groups almost totally dominated the American top twenty. Even Elvis was having difficulty competing with Beatlemania.

In an effort to circumvent the British musical monopoly, Shelby Singleton decided to cut a country album with Jerry Lee. *Country Songs for City Folks* was the result, Jerry's first full-fledged country session. A single was culled from the album, and sales looked very promising. The single titled "Green Green Grass of Home" began a slow but steady climb up the country charts. Almost immediately, though, a young singer in England recorded his own version of the same tune. Tom Jones was the young vocalist, and *his* version of "Green Green Grass of Home" catapulted into *Billboard*'s top ten; Jerry's record faltered and faded. Once again the British monopoly prevailed.

Next came "Memphis Beat" and "Soul My

Showing off gold records for "Another Place, Another Time," "What Made Milwaukee Famous," "She Still Comes Around," and "To Make Love Sweeter for You."

Way," two final attempts to break the British barrier—commendable, but unsuccessful.

In December of 1966, Shelby Singleton resigned his position as head of A & R at Mercury Records to form his own production company. The task of producing Jerry's future product fell on the talented shoulders of young Jerry Kennedy, former studio musician and Shelby's assistant for many years.

Finally, after five frustrating years of attempting to make a serious dent in the pop charts, Jerry Lee and Jerry Kennedy decided to aim all future efforts toward the country field, going back to his southern roots. Actually Jerry's association with country music goes back to 1956 and his very first release on Sun, which was "Crazy Arms," a remake of the old Ray Price hit. The flip side of many of the Killer's biggest rock hits (such as "You Win Again," "Fools Like Me," or "Cold, Cold Heart") were pure country.

To prepare the country stations for his new product, Jerry met and talked with DJs all over the U.S. He told them all his future records would be "pure country," but he would still do his rock 'n' roll hits in his stage act. "So let's get together and quit this 'ban' crap, okay?" Their reaction: "Welcome back, Jerry!"

The first effort by the combined talents of Jerry Kennedy and Jerry Lee Lewis was *Another Place, Another Time*—a smash! The album shot up to number three on the C & W charts, the single (from the album) also went to Number Three. Jerry was back in "hillbilly heaven," at the top of the charts where he belonged.

What followed then was an almost unbroken chain of hit records. "What's Made Milwaukee Famous (Has Made a Loser Out of Me") (Number Two), "She Still Comes Around" (Number Two), "To Make Love Sweeter for You" (Number One), "One Has My Name" (Number Three), "She Even Woke Me Up to Say Goodbye" (Number Two), "Once More with Feeling" (Number Two), "I Can't Seem to Say Goodbye" (Number Seven), "There Must be More to Love Than This" (Number One), "Touching Home" (Number Three), "Chantilly Lace" (Number One), "Middle-Age Crazy" (Number Five), etc.

The Killer was back: bigger than ever—just in another field.

The following is an interview with Jerry Kennedy, who almost single-handedly returned Jerry Lee Lewis to his prominence as a major recording artist in the country field. Between 1968 and 1978, he produced every album Mercury/Phonogram released by Jerry Lee Lewis (except four). This conversation took place in October 1979.

**Robert Cain:**
In 1968 a decision was made to aim Jerry Lee Lewis for the country market. Who made that decision and why was it made?

**Jerry Kennedy:**
Actually, the idea came about in 1966, probably at a place where you wouldn't think that something like that would be decided. A guy by the name of Bobby Denton at that time was program director at WIVK in Knoxville. He and I had the chance to sit together at a hockey game in Knoxville, back when Nashville and Knoxville had hockey teams in the Eastern Hockey League. Bobby approached me at the game, and it was the first time I ever met the guy, and he said: "Why doesn't your company wise up and record Jerry Lee Lewis country?" (At that time we were turning out the rock stuff with Jerry. Shelby Singleton was in charge of his recordings and everything.) And I said: "Hey, man, the guy is really country, but I'm not sure that is where he would want to go." But, anyway, the seed was planted two years before we ever did any country sessions. In 1968 we had a guy at Mercury by the name of Eddie Kilroy, who was the national promotion man. Now this is two years later, he came to me with a song called "Another Place, Another Time," written by Jerry Chestnut. He played the song for me and said: "Why in the hell don't we record this thing with Jerry Lee Lewis?" and I said: "Hey, the guy needs a record: if he's game, we'll give it a shot!"

**Cain:**
What was Jerry's reaction to that particular song?

**Kennedy:**
I think it was something like "I could sing the hell out of it!"

**Cain:**
Were you surprised when your very first effort with Jerry Lee in the country field was a smash hit?

**Kennedy:**
Yes, I think everybody was. We didn't anticipate the total volume that we did on that record by any stretch of the imagination. That record went well over 200,000 singles and up to that point we had been selling in the 30,000 to 75,000 bracket with the rock stuff we were doing, which is bad.

**Cain:**
*Soul My Way* was the first album that carried your name on it with Jerry Lee. Weren't you affiliated with him prior to that?

**Kennedy:**
Yes, as a guitarist on his recordings. In addition to production duties with Mercury during the sixties, I also played guitar on a lot of sessions for other labels. I used to play guitar for Smash or Mercury or whatever labels were affiliated with Mercury.

**Cain:**
I believe that Jerry Lee received Gold Records for "Another Place, Another Time," "What Made Milwaukee Famous," "She Still Comes Around," and "To Make Love Sweeter for You." Did he have any other Gold Records on Mercury to your knowledge?

**Kennedy:**
Those were *not* gold in the sense that R.I.A.A. certified those recordings as gold because in that period you're speaking of, it had to go a million before it was gold. These were Gold Records made up by the record company (Mercury) and presented to Jerry just because of the success that those particular singles had achieved.

**Cain:**
Was this then some sort of promotional stunt?

**Kennedy:**
It was just a gesture on the part of Mercury to Jerry Lee showing their appreciation for having gone "Top Five" or "Number One" or wherever those records went. It was something we had made up. We weren't trying to get any promotion out of the thing at all. There may have been a photo in the trades of us presenting the records to Jerry, but we certainly did not intend for the public to misread that as those records having sold a million each.

**Cain:**
You were listed as the coauthor of "To Make Love Sweeter for You." Had you done other things in the songwriting field?

**Kennedy:**
Not for a long time. I had participated in writing some songs back in the early sixties. Glenn Sutton, who had written "What Made Milwaukee Famous" and "She Still Comes Around," came to me on a day we were going to do a Jerry Lee session at two in the afternoon. He came into my office at eight or nine in the morning and said: "I have a great idea for a song. Can you help me finish it?" And the idea was the song "To Make Love Sweeter for You." He had several lines and a little bit of a melody, and we sat there and finished the thing. I think Jerry got there at one and we recorded it at two.

**Cain:**
That is *fast*!

**Kennedy:**
We were under a lot of pressure. Sometimes pressure can make you do a lot of things you wouldn't do normally. Glenn Sutton, incidentally, is a pressure writer.

**Cain:**
Since you obviously have some talent in that direction, why haven't you pursued it further?

**Kennedy:**
I think you can spread yourself too thin . . . if you're trying to do too many things at one time. I think the guitar playing I was doing on outside sessions, labels other than Mercury, hurt production for some of the records I was doing for Mercury. So I wised up and gave that up—even though I hated to because I love guitar playing. I hung that up and I feel like I am able to concentrate a lot better . . . plus I have always had a theory that I can't write the songs that I produce, although I know a lot of producers do.

With country star Eddie Dean at Country & Western awards show at Hollywood Palladium, May 1979.

**Cain:**
You produced so many hit records for Jerry Lee, are there any that you are particularly fond of?

**Kennedy:**
No, I am proud of *all* the records we had. I can't single out one as being more important or one I like more than another. That would be a little unfair. If anything, circumstances surrounding some sessions will dictate your opinion. I think that the most enjoyable sessions that I did with Jerry were the *Hall of Fame* albums, volume 1 and volume 2. They came so easy. The albums were recorded . . . finished . . . the whole shot in two or three days.

**Cain:**
That's amazing, to produce so much work in such a short time!

**Kennedy:**
When you are working with a talent like he is. . . . Probably half of those songs came on the first take.

**Cain:**
I have spoken to many people in the music business, and most of them refer to Jerry Lee Lewis as a "living legend." Would you agree with that definition?

**Kennedy:**
Yes, there is no way that you could *not* think of Jerry as a "living legend." Hey, who in our industry doesn't know Jerry Lee? To me, a legend is when people say:"Hey man, have you heard any new Jerry Lee Lewis stories?" There are *so many*. You know, people talk—especially in *our* industry—and make him the highlight of conversations at lunch or playing poker or whatever. This is what makes a legend.

**Cain:**
I have been told that on many recordings with Jerry Lee, the person who actually did the piano playing was Pig Robbins.

**Kennedy:**
True. In many instances Jerry would get here thirty minutes before we were ready to go into the studio. Anyone who knows anything about music would know that's a *heavy* situation. When you are throwing some new material at a guy, and he has never heard the songs we are going to record fifteen minutes from now. Jerry would have enough to think about performing vocally with these songs. It was a lot easier to lay down some things if we had Pig Robbins there, and Pig could sit in on piano, and Jerry could concentrate on the vocals.

**Cain:**
You've known Jerry for at least ten years. To your knowledge, does he have any hobbies or interests besides his music?

**Kennedy:**
Not that I know of. I never socialized with Jerry a lot—we never sat down and discussed each other's life-styles, but I do know he loves to watch TV.

**Cain:**
Just recently Jerry's father, Elmo, died. Did you ever meet Elmo, and what was he like?

**Kennedy:**
Like an older version of Jerry Lee. He would sit around and have a few belts with the guys . . . sit around and sing "Shanty in Old Shanty Town." I even spotted some of the places that Jerry might have gotten some of his talent from. Hey, he was an entertainer!

A couple of years ago, at a club here in Nashville, I remember going down to see Jerry Lee perform. We had done some recording earlier that day. Jerry called Elmo up on stage, and he did, I think, "Shanty in Old Shanty Town." He blew the crowd away.

**Cain:**
I've been told that a recording session with Jerry Lee Lewis is like a family reunion. How does it affect your ability to produce a record?

**Kennedy:**
Yes, they were like family reunions, except it was the family who had just left Memphis—I never could understand it. Maybe they all came over in separate cars, but they would all act like it was the first time they had seen each other in a few weeks when they would get together in the studio. They hampered efforts to operate. The control room is a very sacred place to me, and obviously these people could not party out in the studio where the recording was going on, so it did hinder efforts in the control room. We ran into several problems with a little too much noise and things like that. But, hey, with a guy like that you have to respect him for tak-

ing care of the people around him. I'm not sure he needed all those people around him, but he never said a word. It bothered us to the extent that they could get a little noisy at times.

**Cain:**
On the hit record, "I'll Find It Where I Can": it's the only record, to my knowledge, that does not feature the typical Jerry Lee Lewis piano solo on it. Whose idea was that?

**Kennedy:**
That probably fell into place the way that we decided to record the song. Jerry did not play piano on that cut. That was Pig Robbins playing piano on "Find It Where I Can." It was probably a thing where I told Pig we don't want to turn this into a Lewis-sounding record—it's not that kind of song. As well as I remember, we treated it a little different from anything we had done with Jerry before in the studio.

**Cain:**
The reason I ask is because he does not play piano at all when he performs that song on stage.

**Kennedy:**
That's interesting, I didn't know that.

**Cain:**
What was your reaction when you heard they are planning to make a movie from the hit record you and Jerry produced called "Middle-Age Crazy"?

**Kennedy:**
I thought it would be a *fantastic* idea! Probably because of my interest in Sonny Throckmorton as a songwriter, and he's also a Mercury artist. "Middle-Age Crazy" has got to be one of my favorite songs. I've cut a lot of songs, over a bunch of years. When Sonny brought that tune to me, it was probably one of the easiest songs to sit and draw

pictures of. I could just picture this guy: you know, running around with this chick—the cars and the whole thing. I even made a remark to the people before we went downstairs and cut that record that day. I said: "What a hell of a book that would make." I didn't say movie, but we all know that books spawn movies too.

**Cain:**
What was Jerry's reaction to the song? It's not the kind of material he usually does.

**Kennedy:**
His reaction to it was the same as mine: he flipped out over the song. In the past, when we played songs for him, we knew we had good material . . . from "Milwaukee" to whatever. However, this song was a little different, in the sense that I think a lot of people could have done it. But I needed a *great song* for Jerry Lee at that time. To be honest with you, I was apprehensive and was afraid that he would not like it, because it was so different. I was really pleased because he said, "Fantastic!" or something to that effect . . . He jumped up and down, he was so excited. He was as excited as I was when we went in to record it.

**Cain:**
The Jordanaires were added to several of your Lewis recording sessions. How did that come about?

**Kennedy:**
That's through a friendship with the Jordanaires. Gosh, they're a very competent vocal group. Jerry liked the Jordanaires—it made for a pleasant recording session to hire them. They're very professional people, plus the blend is there with his kind of music. You select a vocal group not because you think, hey, these guys need work, or Elvis used these people, or whatever. It's just that I thought this was the best matchup I could get. Sometimes they were augmented with some female singers too.

**Cain:**
There were two albums on Mercury/Phonogram that you did not produce, *Southern Roots* and *1–40 Country*. Why were you not involved in those two?

**Kennedy:**
There were some times during the years that Jerry was with Mercury when I could not agree with some of the people around him. There's one thing I'd like to stress here at this point: Jerry and I never had a cross word. We always had a fantastic relationship. The *Southern Roots* album, if I'm not mistaken, was recorded in Memphis. I don't like to make records outside of Nashville, and that could have been the reason. *1–40 Country:* gosh, I don't know. I know that there was a period when, either from disagreements with some of his management or some of the people around him, I said: "Hey, it would be unfair for me to go in now, number one. I'm busy, and I've got a lot of other acts I'm working with now." Sometimes scheduling had a lot to do with it.

**Cain:**
In the last twelve years, neither Jerry Lee Lewis or Elvis Presley has won even one award from the Country Music Association. Can you give me your opinion on how that could have happened?

**Kennedy:**
The only thing I can say is, I don't understand it. Both of these guys made such a contribution to country music. I'm not sure whether it's a political thing or whether it's an oversight . . . or people thought they were rock 'n' rollers or whatever. Their contributions certainly should have entitled them to be nominated. I'm not sure how those things work, but I've never been able to understand why they haven't won—especially during the late sixties and early seventies. I always thought that Jerry should

have been involved in at least the nominations.

**Cain:**
Certain songs Jerry recorded, like "Boogie-Woogie Country Man," "My Life Would Make a Damn Good Country Song," or "Jerry Lee's Rock 'N' Roll Revival Show," were obviously written just for Jerry Lee Lewis. Isn't that unusual?

**Kennedy:**
Yes, it's unusual and I'd say it's a tribute to Jerry. If you look at the writers on those songs, those guys were having a lot of successes. I think Jerry Foster and Bill Rice wrote "Jerry Lee's Revival Show." Yes, they made a point to sit down and write that one especially for him. I would say it's a tribute to Jerry Lee that they would do this.

**Cain:**
To your knowledge, are there any unreleased records by Jerry at Mercury?

**Kennedy:**
Yes, there are. I believe we have several good sides. I can think of two or three right now. I wouldn't want to reveal the titles at this point, because they could be recut somewhere else. These are sides which were accumulated over a period of years that have not been released. Some of them are very good. There aren't any plans at this time to release any of them.

**Cain:**
Jerry has often said that he prides himself on the ability to record a song in one take or at the most, two takes. Would you say this is generally true?

**Kennedy:**
Yes, in fact we have had a lot of hit records recorded in one take—certainly the balance of them in two. He has a tendency to become tired of a song after he does it four,

five, or six times—unlike other artists. It depends on the people you're recording: some artists get a little better as we go along. I think he gets a little tired of something and starts playing with it. It just doesn't have as much feeling as the first time he lays it down. That is why we always try to keep the musicians on their toes. We tell them, "Hey, when that light goes on, guys, it's for dead serious." It became a habit over the years. We used the same pickers a lot on most of his recordings, and they knew that when we turned that light on, we could be through in two or three minutes!

**Cain:**
Is that unusual or commonplace?

**Kennedy:**
Unusual! Gosh, you read now where people book a studio for three months to record an album. Lewis would laugh if he heard that—it's not typical of the way he works. The key word with Jerry is pride: He has a lot of pride. When he sits down at the piano and the light goes on, that's it. He does not want to go on experimenting at that point.

**Cain:**
Was there ever any attempt to have Jerry record with anyone other than Linda Gail Lewis?

**Kennedy:**
No, he was never approached, at least not through me. Never approached to do any duets with anybody else. I always thought that would be unfair to both people. He is such a stylist: it would be hard to have someone walk into the studio with Jerry Lee Lewis and do a duet with him—they're certainly going to get stepped on!

**Cain:**
Can you name any country artist who in your opinion would look forward to following Jerry Lee Lewis onstage?

**Kennedy:**
I don't know anyone that crazy!

As a result of the Killer's tremendous impact on the country and western market, several honors were bestowed upon him during the early seventies. The first was the invitation to appear at the Grand Ole Opry, Nashville's most prestigious institution. Whatever trepidations he may have had about his reception were soon laid to rest. Introduced by Charlie Walker ("He's been a top star in rock music for years; a top star in country music now"), Jerry played such Lewis favorites as "Another Place, Another Time," "Waiting for a Train," "Me and Bobby McGee," and "Chantilly Lace," and each was greeted with a warm reception. One of the many highlights of his Opry debut was his piano duet with longtime Opry favorite Del Wood. Their rendition of "Down Yonder" was described as "nothing less than brilliant." His performance January 20, 1973, was greeted by rave reviews, four encores, and a standing ovation. For the radio broadcast portion of the show, the last two commercials were dropped to enable Jerry to complete his act without any interruptions.

That same year (on June 2, 1973) he received the Trustees' Award from *Memphis Music* as the Memphis Artist of the Year.

He was also nominated for a Grammy for his Mercury Records chart topper "Chantilly Lace."

After performing a number of benefit shows, Jerry was made an honorary citizen of Huntsville, Alabama, and Hot Springs, Arkansas. During this same period a street was named after him in his hometown of Ferriday, Louisiana—Jerry Lee Lewis Avenue.

Another major event of that period was his appearance in Wembley Stadium, London, England, for a huge rock concert featuring a lineup of the stars that rocked the world during the fabulous fifties: Little Richard, Bill Haley, Bo Diddley, Chuck Berry and, of course, Jerry Lee Lewis. A rousing rock concert with a crowd estimated at 74,000! The entire show was filmed and released as a feature film in the mid-seventies (*London Rock and Roll Show*).

But while his career was soaring to astronomical heights, his personal life became a series of tragedies. In 1970, Jerry's wife of thirteen years, mother of their two children (Steven Allen Lewis, Jr., deceased, and Phoebe Lewis), filed for divorce on grounds of cruelty and infidelity. As the story goes, Myra had hired a private detective to follow Jerry and obtain evidence against him. After the divorce was final, Myra married the detective.

October 1971—One bright spot: Jerry Lee married his fourth wife, the former Jaren Gunn Pate. Jaren had worked for the Memphis Sheriff's Department, and prior to meeting Jerry she had never been associated with show business.

April 1971—Disaster struck again. Jerry's beloved mother, Mary Ethel Lewis, died after a lengthy struggle with cancer. She was only fifty-nine. The intense love and affection Jerry had for his mother was beyond words. Probably the best attempt to describe the deep relationship they shared was made by Frankie Jean Lewis when she said to me, "Jerry *idolized* her, and she *idolized* him." Many people agree that Jerry has never been quite the same person since his mother's death.

November 13, 1973—Young Jerry Lee Lewis, Jr., was killed instantly in a car wreck just outside of Hernando, Mississippi. He was only nineteen years old.

When interviewed by *People* magazine in 1977, Jerry commented, "The loss of my mother and two sons got to me. I was drinking heavy. I needed a fifth of tequila just to sober up. I couldn't cut a record. It wasn't the marriages that brought me down, it was just the passin' of the caskets." But Jerry Lee prevailed, mostly by burying himself deeper and deeper in his music. More re-cording sessions, more night club engagements, more television appearances, more long, grueling road tours. Crisscrossing the country in an endless chain of one-night stands, hoping the sound of applause would drown out the echoes of his sorrow. Sometimes it did.

What is success to Jerry Lee Lewis? Here are his thoughts.

*Success is just a blessing from God, and very few people have it, and even though the people that have it don't know how to accept it and they lose it and even though they become the greatest things in the world, they don't really realize the true value of certain things around them that mean so much, and success is what you make out of it. [He continued,] I'm talking about me now. It's something that you got to learn to handle. Success is something you have to handle . . . and you have to handle it right. Now you can let it get the best of you. I mean, you can become big in the business. People love you—they flock after, they want to be around you . . . see your show . . . everybody wants to talk to you. But it's something that you have to learn to control, and if you can't control it, it'll kill you.*

Success is no stranger to the Killer. Most artists would be happy to be successful in one field. Jerry Lee is one of the handful of performers who have successfully bridged the gap between pop and country music and reached the top in both.

Dick Clark commented on this:

*Lots of interesting things happened to people who became pop-rock stars whose country roots finally came back to serve them in good stead. Jerry Lee Lewis is one, Conway Twitty is another, Carl Perkins is another, even Johnny Cash came and went back to the original. I think it's that secret magic something that we call star power. It doesn't really have anything to do with the kind of music you are singing or selling. Jerry Lee has, first of all, a significant sound unto himself. He is a song stylist, as it were. You know when you hear him it's Jerry Lee Lewis, whether he is singing a country song or some crazy rock 'n' roll song. For a number of reasons, I guess, he has lasted these fifteen years or so.*

The Killer's final session for Mercury produced a touching country ballad titled "Middle-Age Crazy." The lyrics of this song speak to all of us who are over forty, but in particular it says much about Jerry and where he is today.

Today he's forty years old
going on twenty
Don't look for the gray in his hair
'cause he ain't got any
He's middle-age crazy
Trying to prove he still can

The impression that Jerry Lee Lewis has left on popular and country music in his amazing twenty-three-year career is deep, bold, and long-lasting. But Jerry does not live in the past; he constantly looks ahead.

What does the future hold for Jerry Lee? No one can say for certain. He'll probably just keep on being the "World's Oldest Teenager," as he often calls himself—saying what he wants to say, doing just what he wants to do, and "Hanging in Like Gunga Din."

Once Jerry was asked, "Do you think there will ever be anyone else like you?" "I certainly hope so," he replied. "Why?" The Killer paused a moment, then said, "Just think what a dull world this would be without a Jerry Lee Lewis in it."

"Middle-Age Crazy" by Sonny Throckmorton. © 1977 Tree Publishing Company, Inc. Used by permission.

In the den of his ranch at Nesbit, Mississippi.

# Discography

Jerry Lee signed his first recording contract with Sun Records in 1956. The contract was renewed in 1958 and Jerry remained with the Memphis-based label until 1963. Later that year he signed with Smash Records (a division of Mercury). Eventually the Smash label was phased out (1970) and Jerry became a Mercury artist until 1978. In July 1969, Shelby Singleton purchased the entire Sun catalog and changed the name to Sun International. He then began releasing some of the hundreds of songs Jerry recorded for Sam Phillips, which were never released. In 1978, Jerry signed with Electra Records.

## SUN SINGLES

259: Crazy Arms/End of the Road
(Dec. 1956)

● 267: Whole Lotta Shakin' Goin' On/It'll Be Me
(Apr. 1957)

● 281: Great Balls of Fire/You Win Again
(Nov. 1957)

● 288: Breathless/Down the Line
(Feb. 1958)

● 296: High School Confidential/Fools Like Me
(May 1958)

301: The Return of Jerry Lee (narration by George Klein)/Lewis Boogie
(June 1958)

303: Breakup/I'll Make It All Up to You
(Aug. 1958)

312: I'll Sail My Ship Alone/It Hurt Me So
(Nov. 1958)

317: Lovin' Up a Storm/Big Blon' Baby
(Feb. 1959)

NOTE: ● Bullet indicates single which has sold a million copies

324: Let's Talk About Us/Ballad of Billy Joe
(June 1959)

330: Little Queenie/ I Could Never Be Ashamed of You
(Sept. 1959)

337: Old Black Joe/Baby, Baby, Bye Bye
(Mar. 1960)

344: John Henry/Hang Up My Rock 'n' Roll Shoes
(Aug. 1960)

352: When I Get Paid/Love Made a Fool of Me
(Nov. 1960)

356: What'd I Say/Livin' Lovin' Wreck
(Feb. 1961)

364: Cold, Cold Heart/It Won't Happen with Me
(June 1961)

367: Save the Last Dance for Me/As Long as I Live
(Sept. 1961)

371: Money/Bonnie B.
(Nov. 1961)

374: I've Been Twistin'/Ramblin' Rose
(Jan. 1962)

379: Sweet Little Sixteen/How's My Ex Treating You
(July 1962)

382: Good Golly Miss Molly/I Can't Trust Me in Your Arms Anymore
(Nov. 1962)

384: Teenage Letter/Seasons of My Heart (with Linda Gail Lewis)
(Apr. 1963)

396: Carry Me Back to Old Virginia/I Know What It Means
(Mar. 1965)

## SUN EPs

107: That Great Ball of Fire/Mean Woman Blues/I'm Feeling Sorry/Turn Around/Whole Lotta Shakin'
(1957)

108: Jerry Lee Lewis No. 1: Don't Be Cruel/Good Night, Irene/Put Me Down/It All Depends
(1958)

109: Jerry Lee Lewis No. 2: Ubangi Stomp/Crazy Arms/Jambalaya/Fools Like Me
(1958)

110: Jerry Lee Lewis No. 3: High School Confidential/When the Saints Go Marching In/Matchbox/It'll Be Me (different take from the single version on Sun 267)
(1958)

**SMASH RECORDS** THE GOLDEN HITS OF **Jerry Lee Lewis**

WHOLE LOTTA SHAKIN' GOIN' ON
GREAT BALLS OF FIRE
BREATHLESS
CRAZY ARMS
YOU WIN AGAIN
YOUR CHEATING HEART
FOOLS LIKE ME
DOWN THE LINE
BREAK-UP
I'LL MAKE IT UP TO YOU
HIGH SCHOOL CONFIDENTIAL
END OF THE ROAD

The first album on the Smash label.

## SUN ALBUMS
Sun 1230: *Jerry Lee Lewis*
Don't Be Cruel/Good Night, Irene/Put Me Down/It All Depends/Ubangi Stomp/Crazy Arms/Jambalaya/Fools Like Me/High School Confidential/When the Saints Go Marching In/Matchbox/It'll Be Me* (*different take from the single version on Sun 267)
(1958)

Sun 1265: *Jerry Lee's Greatest*
Money/As Long as I Live/Frankie and Johnny/Home/Hello, Hello, Baby/Country Music Is Here to Stay/Let's Talk About Us/What'd I Say/Breakup/Great Balls of Fire/Cold, Cold Heart/Hello, Josephine
(1961)

Sun 1250: *Sun Million Sellers*
(various artists)
Whole Lotta Shakin' Goin' On/You Win Again/Breathless
(1961)

## PHILLIPS INTERNATIONAL
(a division of Sun)
Single PI 3559: In the Mood/I Get the Blues When It Rains (issued under pseudonym "The Hawk")
(Jan. 1960)

## SUN INTERNATIONAL "GOLDEN TREASURE" SERIES
Singles:
14: Crazy Arms/End of the Road
18: Whole Lotta Shakin'/It'll Be Me (same version as on Sun 102)
21: Great Balls of Fire/You Win Again
25: Breathless/Down the Line
28: High School Confidential/Fools Like Me
29: Lewis Boogie/Return of Jerry Lee
31: Breakup/I'll Make It All Up to You
34: I'll Sail My Ship Alone/It Hurt Me So
36: Lovin' Up a Storm/Big Blon' Baby

38: Let's Talk About Us/Ballad of Billy Joe
39: Little Queenie/I Could Never Be Ashamed of You
42: Old Black Joe/Baby, Baby, Bye Bye
44: John Henry/Hang Up My Rock 'n' Roll Shoes
46: When I Get Paid/Love Made a Fool of Me
48: What'd I Say/Livin' Lovin' Wreck
50: It Won't Happen with Me/Cold, Cold Heart
51: Save the Last Dance for Me/As Long as I Live
52: Money/Bonnie B.
53: I've Been Twistin'/Ramblin' Rose (same version as on Sun 108)
55: How's My Ex Treating You/Sweet Little Sixteen (same version as on Sun 107)
56: Good Golly Miss Molly/I Can't Trust Me in Your Arms Anymore
57: Teenage Letter/Seasons of My Heart (with Linda Gail Lewis)
59: Carry Me Back to Old Virginia/I Know What It Means

NOTE: According to Shelby Singleton, all of the above Golden Treasure Singles were released at the same time—July 1979.

## SUN INTERNATIONAL "REGULAR" SERIES
Singles:
1101: Invitation to Your Party/I Could Never Be Ashamed of You (1969)
1107: One Minute Past Eternity/Frankie and Johnny (1969)
1115: I Can't Seem to Say Goodbye/Good Night, Irene (1970)
1119: Waiting for a Train/Big-Legged Woman (1970)
1125: Love on Broadway/Matchbox (1971)

1128: Your Lovin' Ways/I Can't Trust Me in Your Arms Anymore (1972)

1130: I Can't Trust Me in Your Arms Anymore/Good Rockin' To-night (1973)

1138: Matchbox/Am I To Be the One (1978)

1139: Save the Last Dance for Me/Am I To Be the One (vocal duets) (1978)

1141: Cold, Cold Heart/Hello, Josephine (vocal duets) (1979)

## SUN INTERNATIONAL ALBUMS

Sun 102: *Original Golden Hits*
Volume I
Crazy Arms/You Win Again/Lewis Boogie/Great Balls of Fire/Down the Line/End of The Road/Little Queenie/Teenage Letter/Whole Lotta Shakin'/Breathless/It'll Be Me (1969)

Sun 103: *Original Golden Hits*
Volume 2
Fools Like Me/I'll Sail My Ship Alone/How's My Ex Treating You/Money/High School Confidential/I Could Never Be Ashamed of You/Save the Last Dance For Me/Mean Woman Blues/Breakup/I'll Make It All Up to You/What'd I Say (1969)

Sun 107: *Rocking Rhythm and Blues*
C. C. Rider/What'd I Say/Little Queenie/Big-Legged Woman/Good Rockin' Tonight/Good Golly Miss Molly/Save the Last Dance for Me/Sweet Little Sixteen/Hang Up My Rock 'n' Roll Shoes/Hello, Josephine/Johnny B. Goode (1969)

Sun 108: *Golden Cream of the Country*
Invitation to Your Party/Cold, Cold Heart/Ramblin' Rose/One Minute Past Eternity/Frankie and Johnny/Home/Jambalaya/How's My Ex Treating You/Seasons of My Heart (with Linda Gail)/I Can't Trust Me in Your Arms Anymore/As Long as I Live (1969)

Sun 114: *A Taste of Country*
I Can't Seem To Say Good-bye/I Love You So Much It Hurts/I'm Throwing Rice/Good Night, Irene/Your Cheating Heart/Am I To Be the One (with Charlie Rich)/Crazy Arms/Night Train to Memphis/As Long as I Live/You Win Again/It Hurt Me So (1970)

Sun 119: *Sunday Down South*
(other tracks by Johnny Cash)
Will the Circle Be Unbroken/Old Time Religion/Carry Me Back to Old Virginia/When the Saints Go Marching In/Silver Threads (1971)

Sun 121: *Ole Tyme Country Music*
All Around the Water Tank/Carry Me Back to Old Virginia/John Henry/Old Black Joe/My Blue Heaven/You're the Only Star in My Blue Heaven/Crawdad Song/Hand Me Down My Walking Cane/You Are My Sunshine/If the World Keeps on Turning/Deep Elem Blues (1970)

Sun 124: *Monsters*
Don't Be Cruel/Your Cheatin' Heart/Save the Last Dance for Me/Pink Pedal Pushers/Good Golly Miss Molly/Matchbox/Be Bop a Lula/Jailhouse Rock/Drinkin' Wine Spo-dee-o-dee/Honey Hush/Singing the Blues (1971)

Sun 125: *Johnny Cash and Jerry Lee Lewis Sing Hank Williams*
(other tracks by Johnny Cash)
Lovesick Blues/You Win Again/Your Cheatin' Heat/Jambalaya/Setting the Woods on Fire (1971)

The first "live" album Jerry Lee ever recorded.

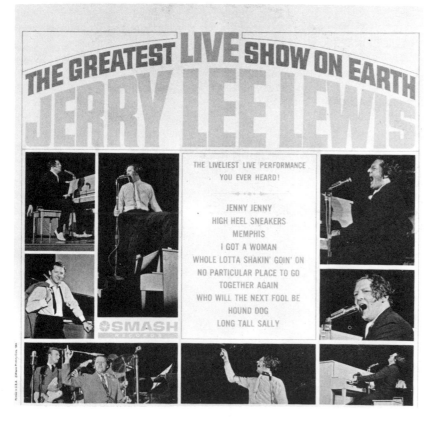

Sun 128: *Original Golden Hits*
    Volume 3
One Minute Past Eternity/Let's Talk About Us/Your Lovin' Ways/I Can't Trust Me in Your Arms Anymore/Lovin' Up a Storm/Love on Broadway/Sweet Little Sixteen (same version as Sun 107)/Invitation to Your Party/I Love You Because/As Long as I Live/Good Golly Miss Molly (1971)

Sun 1000: *Golden Rock & Roll*
Whole Lotta Twistin'/Rock and Roll Ruby/Sick and Tired/When I Get Paid/The Return of Jerry Lee/Milk Shake Mademoiselle/Pumping Piano Rock/Let the Good Times Roll/Livin' Lovin' Wreck/Feel So Good/High-Powered Woman/Hello, Hello, Baby/My Bonnie/Ubangi Stomp/Hong Kong Blues/I've Been Twistin'/Ooby, Dooby/My Quadroon/Rockin' the Boat of Love/Lewis Boogie (1977)

Sun 1005: *The Original Jerry Lee Lewis*
Crazy Arms/End of the Road/It'll Be Me/Whole Lotta Shakin' Goin' On/You Win Again/Great Balls of Fire/Down the Line/Breathless/High School Confidential/Fools Like Me/Breakup/I'll Make It All Up to You/Lovin' Up a Storm/Big Blon' Baby/Livin' Lovin' Wreck/What'd I Say (1978)

Sun 1011: *Duets* (Jerry Lee Lewis and Friends)
Save the Last Dance for Me/Sweet Little Sixteen/I Love You Because/C. C. Rider/Am I To Be the One/Sail Away/Cold, Cold Heart/Hello, Josephine/It Won't Happen with Me/What'd I Say/Good Golly Miss Molly (1978)

Sun 1018: *Trio + Friends* Jerry Lee Lewis, Charlie Rich, Carl Perkins, and Friends
Be Bop a Lula/On My Knees/Dixie Fried/Gentle as a Lamb/Money/Breakup/Matchbox/Good Rockin' Tonight/Gone, Gone, Gone/Sittin' and Thinkin' (1979)

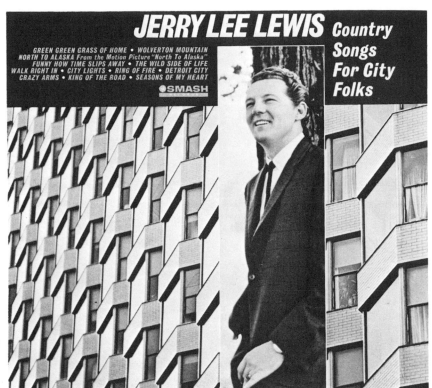

His first country album for Smash, produced by Shelby Singleton. Contains "The Green Green Grass of Home," which Tom Jones later recorded.

**ALL TIME SMASH HITS SERIES**
Singles:
Smash S1412: Whole Lotta Shakin' Goin' On/Breathless (Jan. 1965)

S1413: Great Balls of Fire/High School Confidential (Jan. 1965)

**COUNTRY CELEBRITY SERIES**
Singles:
Smash CC

35020: Another Place, Another Time/What's Made Milwaukee Famous (1970)

35021: She Still Comes Around/To Make Love Sweeter for You (1970)

35022: Don't Let Me Cross Over/Roll Over, Beethoven (both with Linda Gail Lewis) (1970)

35023: One Has My Name/She Even Woke Me Up to Say Goodbye (1970)

35028: Would You Take Another Chance on Me/Touching Home (1972)

35029: There Must Be More to Love Than This/When He Walks on You (1972)

35034: Who's Gonna Play This Old Piano/Chantilly Lace (1973)

35044: Middle-Age Crazy/I'll Find It Where I Can (1978)

**SMASH**
Regular Singles:
1857: Hit the Road, Jack/Pen and Paper (Oct. 1963)

This album, recorded in 1968, put him back into the Top Ten in the Country field. It was the first album produced by Jerry Kennedy.

1886: I'm on Fire/Bread and Butter Man
(Feb. 1964)

1906: She Was My Baby/The Hole He Said He'd Dig for Me
(June 1964)

1930: High Heel Sneakers/You Went Back on Your Word
(Sept. 1964)

1969: Baby, Hold Me Close/I Believe in You
(Jan. 1965)

1992: Rockin' Pneumonia and the Boogie-Woogie Flu/This Must Be the Place
(June 1965)

2006: Green Green Grass of Home/Baby, You've Got What It Takes (with Linda Gail Lewis)
(Sept. 1965)

2027: Sticks and Stones/What a Heck of a Mess
(Mar. 1966)

2053: Memphis Beat/If I Had It All to Do Over
(Aug. 1966)

2103: It's A Hang-up, Baby/Holding On
(June 1967)

2122: Turn On Your Lovelight/Shotgun Man
(Sept. 1967)

2146: Another Place, Another Time/Walkin' the Floor over You
(Feb. 1968)

2164: What's Made Milwaukee Famous/All the Good Is Gone
(May 1968)

2186: She Still Comes Around/Slippin' Around
(Sept. 1968)

2202: To Make Love Sweeter for You/Let's Talk About Us
(Nov. 1968)

2220: Don't Let Me Cross Over/We Live in Two Different Worlds (both with Linda Gail Lewis)
(Apr. 1969)

2224: One Has My Name/I Can't Stop Loving You
(Apr. 1969)

2244: She Even Woke Me Up to Say Goodbye/Echoes
(Sept. 1969)

2254: Roll Over, Beethoven/Secret Places (both with Linda Gail Lewis)
(Nov. 1969)

2257: Once More with Feeling/You Went Out of Your Way
(Dec. 1969)

## MERCURY SINGLES

73099: There Must Be More to Love Than This/Home Away from Home
(July 21, 1970)

73155: I Can't Have a Merry Christmas, Mary (Without You)/In Loving Memories
(1970)

73192: Touching Home/Woman, Woman
(1971)

73227: When He Walks on You/Foolish Kind of Man
(1971)

73248: Would You Take Another Chance on Me/Me and Bobby McGee
(1971)

73273: Chantilly Lace/Think About It, Darlin'
(Feb. 7, 1972)

73296: Lonely Weekends/Turn on Your Lovelight
(May 18, 1972)

73303: Me and Jesus/Handwriting on the Wall (both with Linda Gail Lewis)
(June 23, 1972)

73328: Who's Gonna Play This Old Piano/No Honky-Tonks in Heaven
(Sept. 7, 1972)

73361: No More Hanging On/The Mercy of a Letter (Jan. 18, 1973)

73374: Drinkin' Wine Spo-dee-o-dee/Rock Medley (1973)

73402: No Headstone on My Grave/Jack Daniel's (Old Number Seven) (1973)

73423: Sometimes a Memory Ain't Enough/I Need to Pray (Aug. 29, 1973)

73462: Just a Little Bit/Meat Man (Feb. 18, 1974)

73491: Telltale Signs/Cold, Cold Morning Light (May 9, 1974)

73618: He Can't Fill My Shoes/Tomorrow's Taking Baby Away (Sept. 9, 1974)

73661: I Can Still Hear the Music in the Restroom/(Remember Me) I'm the One Who Loves You (Jan. 23, 1975)

73685: Boogie-Woogie Country Man/I'm Still Jealous of You (May 12, 1975)

73729: A Damn Good Country Song/When I Take My Vacation in Heaven (Oct. 30, 1975)

73763: Don't Boogie-Woogie/That Kind of Fool (Jan. 14, 1976)

73822: Let's Put It Back Together Again/Jerry Lee's Rock 'n' Roll Revival Show (June 30, 1976)

73872: The Closest Thing to You/You Belong to Me (Nov. 23, 1976)

55011: Middle-Age Crazy/Georgia on My Mind (Oct. 12, 1977)

55021: Come On In/Who's Sorry Now (Feb. 22, 1978)

55028: I'll Find It Where I Can/Don't Let the Stars Get in Your Eyes (May 31, 1978)

**SMASH ALBUMS**

SRS 67040: *The Golden Hits of Jerry Lee Lewis*

Whole Lotta Shakin' Goin' On/Fools Like Me/Great Balls of Fire/I'll Make It All Up to You/Down the Line/End of the Road/Breathless/Crazy Arms/You Win Again/High School Confidential/Breakup/Your Cheatin' Heart (1964)

SRS 67056: *The Greatest Live Show On Earth*

Jenny, Jenny/Who Will the Next Fool Be/Memphis/Hound Dog/I Got a Woman/High Heel Sneakers/No Particular Place to Go/Together Again/Long Tall Sally/Whole Lotta Shakin' Goin' On (Live Album) (1964)

SRS 67063: *The Return of Rock*

I Believe in You/Maybelline/Flip, Flop, and Fly/Roll Over, Beethoven/Don't Let Go/Herman the Hermit/Baby, Hold Me Close/You Went Back on Your Word/Corinna, Corinna/Sexy Ways/Johnny B. Goode/Got You on My Mind (1965)

SRS 67071: *Country Songs for City Folks*

Green Green Grass of Home/Wolverton Mountain/Funny How Time Slips Away/North to Alaska (with Linda Gail Lewis)/The Wild Side of Life/Walk Right In/City Lights/Ring of Fire/Detroit City/Crazy Arms/King of the Road/Seasons of My Heart (1965)

SRS 67079: *Memphis Beat*

Memphis Beat/Mathilda/Drinkin' Wine Spo-dee-o-dee/Hallelujah I Love Her So/She Thinks I Still Care/Just Because/Sticks and Stones/Whenever You're Ready/Lincoln Limousine/Big Boss Man/Too Young/The Urge (1966)

One of the rare occasions when he recorded with someone else.

---

SRS 67086: *By Request* (More of the Greatest Live Show on Earth)
Little Queenie/How's My Ex Treating You/Johnny B. Goode/Green Green Grass of Home/What'd I Say (Part 2)/You Win Again/I'll Sail My Ship Alone/Crying Time/Money/Roll Over, Beethoven (Live Album)
(1967)

SRS 67097: *Soul My Way*
Turn on Your Lovelight/It's A Hangup, Baby/Dream Baby/Just Dropped In/Wedding Bells/He Took It Like a Man/Hey, Baby/Treat Her Right/Holdin' On/Shotgun Man/I Betcha Gonna Like It
(Aug. 24, 1967)

SRS 67104: *Another Place, Another Time*
What's Made Milwaukee Famous/Play Me a Song I Can Cry To/On the Back Row/Walkin' the Floor over You/All Night Long/I'm a

Lonesome Fugitive/Another Place, Another Time/Break My Mind/Before the Next Teardrop Falls/All the Good Is Gone/We Live in Two Different Worlds (with Linda Gail Lewis)
(Apr. 19, 1968)

SRS 67112: *She Still Comes Around* (To Love What's Left of Me)
To Make Love Sweeter for You/Let's Talk About Us/I Can't Get over You/Out of My Mind/Today I Started Loving You Again/She Still Comes Around/Louisiana Man/Release Me/Listen, They're Playing My Song/There Stands the Glass/Echoes
(Nov. 25, 1968)

SRS 67117: *Jerry Lee Lewis Sings the Country Music Hall of Fame*
Volume 1
I Wonder Where You Are Tonight/I'm a

So Lonesome I Could Cry/Jambalaya/Four Walls/Heartaches By the Number/Mom and Dad's Waltz/Sweet Dreams/Born to Lose/Oh, Lonesome Me/You've Still Got a Place in My Heart/I Love You Because/Jackson (with Linda Gail Lewis)
(Apr. 1969)

SRS 67118: *Jerry Lee Lewis Sings Country Music Hall of Fame*
Volume 2
I Can't Stop Loving You/Fräulein/He'll Have to Go/More and More/Why Don't You Love Me (Like You Used to Do)/It Makes No Difference Now/Pick Me Up on Your Way Down/One Has My Name/ I Get the Blues When It Rains/Cold, Cold Heart/Burning Memories/Sweet Thang (with Linda Gail Lewis)
(Apr. 1969)

SRS 67126: *Together: Jerry Lee Lewis and Linda Gail Lewis*
Milwaukee, Here I Come/Jackson/Don't Take It Out on Me/Crying Time/Sweet Thang/Secret Places/Don't Let Me Cross Over/Gotta Travel On/We Live in Two Different Worlds/Earth Up Above/Roll Over, Beethoven
(Aug. 6, 1969)

SRS 67128: *She Even Woke Me Up to Say Goodbye*
Once More with Feeling/Working Man Blues/Waiting for a Train/Brown-Eyed Handsome Man/My Only Claim to Fame/Since I Met You, Baby/She Even Woke Me Up to Say Goodbye/Wine Me Up/When the Grass Grows Over Me/You Went Out of Your Way (To Walk on Me)/Echoes
(Dec. 22, 1969)

SRS 67131: *The Best of Jerry Lee Lewis*
What's Made Milwaukee Famous/Another Place, Another Time/She Even Woke Me Up to Say Goodbye/Louisiana Man/Slippin' Around/All the Good Is Gone/To Make Love Sweeter for You/

The only album cover featuring photos of Jerry Lee, Linda Gail, and Jerry Lee Lewis, Jr., now deceased.

One Has My Name/She Still Comes Around/Once More with Feeling/Let's Talk About Us
(Mar. 3, 1970)

MERCURY ALBUMS

SR 61278: *Live at the International Las Vegas*
She Even Woke Me Up to Say Goodbye/Jambalaya/She Still Comes Around/Drinkin' Champagne/San Antonio Rose/Once More with Feeling/When You Wore a Tulip (with Linda Gail Lewis)/Ballad of Forty Dollars/Flip, Flop, and Fly/Take These Chains from My Heart (sung by Linda Gail Lewis)
(Live Album)
(July 2, 1970)

SR 61318: *In Loving Memories* (Jerry Lee Lewis Gospel Album)
In Loving Memories/The Lily of the Valley/Gather 'Round, Children/My God's Not Dead/He Looked Beyond My Fault/The Old Rugged Cross/I'll Fly Away/I'm Longing for Home/I Know that Jesus Will Be There (duet with Linda Gail Lewis)/Too Much to Gain to Lose/Medley: If We Never Meet Again and I'll Meet You in the Morning
(Nov. 9, 1970)

SR 61323: *There Must Be More to Love than This*
There Must Be More to Love than This/Bottles and Barstools/Reuben James/I'd Be Talkin' All the Time/One More Time/Sweet Georgia Brown/Woman, Woman (Get Out of Our Way)/I Forgot More than You'll Ever Know/Fool-Aid/Home Away from Home/Life's Little Ups and Downs
(Nov. 12, 1970)

SR 61343: *Touching Home*
When He Walks on You (Like You Have Walked on Me)/Time Changes Everything/Help Me Make It Through the Night/Mother, the Queen of My Heart/Hearts Were Made for Beating/Foolish Kind of Man/Touching Home/Please Don't Talk About Me When I'm Gone/You

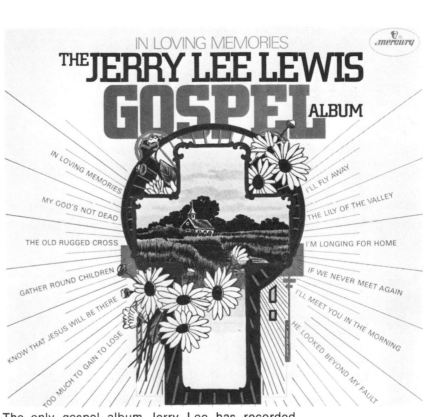

IN LOVING MEMORIES
THE JERRY LEE LEWIS GOSPEL ALBUM

IN LOVING MEMORIES
MY GOD'S NOT DEAD
THE OLD RUGGED CROSS
GATHER ROUND CHILDREN
KNOW THAT JESUS WILL BE THERE
TOO MUCH TO GAIN TO LOSE
I'LL FLY AWAY
THE LILY OF THE VALLEY
I'M LONGING FOR HOME
IF WE NEVER MEET AGAIN
I'LL MEET YOU IN THE MORNING
HE LOOKED BEYOND MY FAULT

The only gospel album Jerry Lee has recorded, produced by Jerry Lee and Linda Gail Lewis. Also features the voice of his mother, Mary Ethel Lewis.

Helped Me Up (When the World Let Me Down)/When Baby Gets the Blues/Comin' Back for More

SR 61346: *Would You Take Another Chance on Me*
Would You Take Another Chance on Me/Another Hand Shaking Goodbye/Swinging Doors/Thirteen at the Table/Big Blon' Baby/Lonesome Fiddle-Man/Me and Bobby McGee/For the Good Times/Things That Matter Most/The Hurtin' Part/Good-bye of the Year
(Oct. 1, 1971)

SRM 1-637: *The Killer Rocks On*
Don't Be Cruel/You Can Have Her/Games People Play/Lonely Weekends/You Don't Miss Your Water/C.C. Rider/Walk a Mile in My Shoes/I'm Walkin'/Me and Bobby McGee/Chantilly Lace/Shotgun Man/Turn On Your Lovelight
(Mar. 15, 1972)

SR 61366: *Who's Gonna Play This Old Piano* (Think About It, Darlin')
Who's Gonna Play This Old Piano/She's Reachin' for My Mind/Too Many Rivers/We Both Know Which One of Us Was Wrong/Wall Around Heaven/No More Hanging On/Think About It, Darlin'/Bottom Dollar/No Traffic Out of Abilene/Parting Is Such Sweet Sorrow/The Mercy of a Letter
(Dec. 15, 1972)

SRM 2-803: *The Session* (Double Album)
Drinkin' Wine Spo-dee-o-dee/Music to the Man/Baby, What You Want Me to Do/Bad Moon Rising/Sea Cruise/Jukebox/No Headstone on My Grave/Big Boss Man/Pledging My Love/Memphis/Trouble in Mind/Johnny B. Goode/High School Confidential (instrumental)/Early

The first double album he produced, released in England in 1973. Includes the hit single "Drinkin' Wine Spo-dee-o-dee."

Morning Rain/Whole Lotta Shakin'/Sixty-Minute Man/Movin' On Down the Line/What'd I Say/Medley: Good Golly Miss Molly—Long Tall Sally—Jenny, Jenny—Tutti Fruitti—Whole Lotta Shakin' (Recorded in England)
(Feb. 15, 1973)

SRM 1-677: *Sometimes a Memory Ain't Enough*
Sometimes a Memory Ain't Enough/Ride Me Down Easy/Mama's Hands/What My Woman Can't Do Can't Be Done/My Cricket and Me/I'm Left, You're Right, She's Gone/Honky-Tonk Wine/Falling to the Bottom/I Need to Pray/The Morning After Baby Let Me Down/Keep Me from Blowing Away
(Sept. 1, 1973)

SRM 1-690: *Southern Roots*
Meat Man/When a Man Loves a Woman/Hold On, I'm Comin'/Just a Little Bit/Born to Be a Loser/Haunted House/Blueberry Hill/The Rev-olutionary Man/Big Blue Diamonds/That Old Bourbon Street Church
(Nov. 15, 1973)

SRM 1-710: *1–40 Country*
He Can't Fill My Shoes/Telltale Signs/A Picture from Life's Other Side/I Hate Good-byes/I've Forgot More About You (Than He'll Ever Know)/Tomorrow's Taking Baby Away/Cold, Cold Morning Light/The Alcohol of Fame/Where Would I Be/Bluer Words/Room Full of Roses
(Apr. 10, 1974)

SRM 1–1030: *Boogie-Woogie Country Man*
I'm Still Jealous of You/A Little Peace and Harmony/Jesus Is on the Main Line/Forever Forgiving/(Remember Me) I'm the One Who Loves You/Red Hot Memories/I Can Still Hear the Music in the Rest-room/Love Inflation/I Was Sorta Wonderin'/Thanks for Nothing/Boogie-Woogie Country Man
(Feb. 28, 1975)

SRM 1-1064: *Odd Man In*
Don't Boogie Woogie (When You Say Your Prayers Tonight)/Shake, Rattle, and Roll/You Ought to See My Mind/I Don't Want to Be Lonely Tonight/That Kind of Fool/Good Night, Irene/A Damn Good Country Song/Jerry's Place/When I Take My Vacation in Heaven/Crawdad Song/Your Cheatin' Heart
(Dec. 15, 1975)

SRM 1-1097: Original Soundtrack *Slumber Party '57* Various Artists
Sh-Boom (The Crew Cuts)/Great Balls of Fire (Jerry Lee Lewis)/Running Bear (Johnny Preston)/Hey! Baby (Bruce Channel)/Breathless (Jerry Lee Lewis)/One Summer Night (the Danleers)/Hey, Paula (Paul and Paula)/Breaking Up Is Hand to Do (Jivin' Gene)/Sea of Love (Phil Phillips)/My Boyfriend's Back (the Angels)/The Great Pretender (the Platters)/Chantilly Lace (the Big Bopper)
(Aug. 16, 1976)

SRM 1-1109: *Country Class*
Let's Put It Back Together Again/No One Will Ever Know/You Belong to Me/I Sure Miss Those Good Old Times/The Old Country Church/After the Fool You've Made of Me/Jerry Lee's Rock 'n' Roll Revival Show/Wedding Bells/Only Love Can Get You in My Door/The One Rose That's Left in My Heart/The Closest Thing to You
(Sept. 20, 1976)

SRM 1-5004: *Country Memories*
Middle-Age Crazy/Let's Say Good-bye Like We Said Hello (In a Friendly Kind of Way)/Who's Sorry Now/Jealous Heart/Georgia on My Mind/Come on In/As Long as We Live/You'd Think by Now I'd Be Over You/Country Memories/What's So Good About Good-bye/Tennessee Saturday Night
(Oct. 17, 1977)

SRM 1-5010: *Jerry Lee Lewis Keeps Rockin'*
I'll Find It Where I Can/Blue Suede Shoes/I Hate You/Arkansas See-

saw/Lucille/The Last Cheater's Waltz/Wild and Wooly Ways/Sweet Little Sixteen/Don't Let the Stars Get in Your Eyes/Pee Wee's Place/Before the Night Is Over
(June 26, 1978)

SRM 1-5006: *The Best of Jerry Lee Lewis Volume 2*
Chantilly Lace/Think About It, Darlin'/Sweet Georgia Brown/Touching Home/Would You Take Another Chance on Me/There Must Be More to Love than This/Middle-Age Crazy/Me and Bobby McGee/Let's Put It Back Together Again/Who's Gonna Play This Old Piano/The Closest Thing to You/Boogie-Woogie Country Man
(Jan. 16, 1978)

SR 61375: *Nashville Package of Original Country Hits* (Various Artists)
What's Made Milwaukee Famous/Another Place, Another Time
(1974)

SR 61372: *Solid Gold Rock 'n' Roll Volume 2* (Various Artists)
Great Balls of Fire
(1971)

## FOREIGN MERCURY ALBUMS

Phillips: SBL 7646: *Live at the Star Club Hamburg*
I Gotta Woman/High School Confidential/Money/Matchbox/What'd I Say, Parts 1 & 2/Great Balls of Fire/Good Golly Miss Molly/Lewis Boogie/Your Cheatin' Heart/Hound Dog/Long Tall Sally/Whole Lotta Shakin'

(Live album recorded in Germany)
(Apr. 1965)

Mercury: *I'm On Fire*
SMCL 20156:
Memphis Beat/Pen and Paper/I'm on Fire/She Was My Baby/This Must Be the Place/What a Heck of a Mess/Rocking Pneumonia & Boogie-Woogie Flu/If I Had to Do It All Over/Hit the Road, Jack/The Hole He Said He'd Dig for Me/Bread and Butter Man/You've Got What It Takes (Duet with Linda Gail Lewis)
(Sept. 1969)

Mercury: *6338-148: Live at the International, Las Vegas*
She Even Woke Me Up to Say Goodbye/Jambalaya/She Still Comes Around/Drinkin' Champagne/San Antonio Rose/Once More with Feeling/When You Wore a Tulip (with Linda Gail Lewis)/Ballad of Forty Dollars/Flip, Flop, and Fly/Take These Chains from My Heart (sung by Linda Gail Lewis)/I Can't Have a Merry Christmas, Mary, Without You/Down the Line
(July 1973)

*6336-300: Rockin' with Jerry Lee Lewis*
Whole Lotta Shakin' Goin' On/Brown-eyed Handsome Man/Corinna, Corinna/High Heel Sneakers/Maybelline/Great Balls of Fire/Johnny B. Goode/Sticks and Stones/Jenny, Jenny/Roll Over, Beethoven/Memphis/High School Confidential
(Released in Holland)
(Apr. 1972)

134-547 MFY: *Let's Rock with Jerry Lee Lewis*
Whole Lotta Shakin' Goin' On/Fools Like Me/Great Balls of Fire/I'll Make It All Up to You/Down the Line/End of the Road/Breathless/Crazy Arms/You Win Again/High School Confidential/Breakup/Your Cheatin' Heart
(1964)

134-215 MCY: *Jerry Lee Lewis Alabama Show*
Jenny, Jenny/Who Will the Next Fool Be/Memphis/Hound Dog/I Got a Wo-Woman/High Heel Sneakers/No Particular Place to Go/Together Again/Long Tall Sally/Whole Lotta Shakin' Goin' On
(Jan. 1965)

1973 album produced in Memphis by Huey Meaux. Features Carl Perkins, Tony Joe White, Mark Lindsay (of Paul Revere and the Raiders), and Jerry Lee Lewis, Jr.

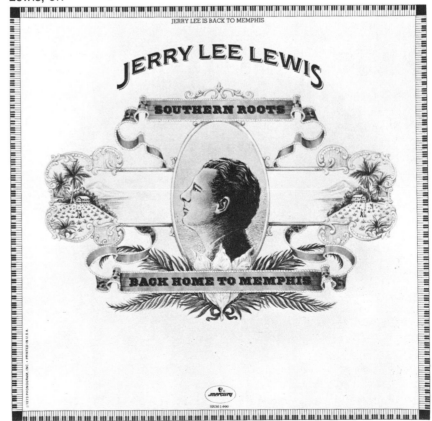

843-454 BY: *The Return of Rock: Jerry Lee Lewis*
I Believe in You/Maybelline/Flip, Flop, and Fly/Roll Over, Beethoven/Don't Let Go/Herman the Hermit/Baby Hold Me Close/You Went Back on Your Word/Corinna, Corinna/Sexy Ways/Johnny B. Goode/Got You on My Mind
(July 1965)

**SUN FOREIGN ALBUMS**
(Released in England on the Charly label)

CR 300 06: *Rare Jerry Lee Lewis Volume 1*
Sixty-Minute Man/Release Me/Sick and Tired/Let the Good Times Roll/Slipping Around/Little Green Valley/So Long, Good-bye/Crazy Heart/Set My Heart at Ease/I Know What It Means/High-Powered Woman/Billy Boy/Wild Side of Life/

When My Blue Moon Turns to Gold Again(Instrumental)/My Quadroon
(1975)

CR 300 007: *Rare Jerry Lee Lewis Volume 2*
Mexicali Rose/That Lucky Old Sun/Ole Pal of Yesterday/All Night Long/Come What May/I Don't Love Nobody/Tomorrow Night/Shame on You/Carolina Sunshine Girl (Instrumental)/I Forgot to Remember to Forget/No More Than I Get/Nothin' Shakin'/Just Who Is to Blame/Born to Lose/Long Gone Lonesome Blues
(1975)

CR 300 02: *Jerry Lee Lewis and His Pumping Piano*
Friday Nights/Wild One (Real Wild Child)/Whole Lot of Twistin'/Dixie (instrumental)/Rock and Roll Ruby/Carry On/Sail Away/Pumpin' Piano Rock/Hound Dog/Hong Kong

Blues/Rocking the Boat of Love/Near You/Cool, Cool Ways/Ooby, Dooby/Someday/Shanty Town
(1975)

CR 301 11: *The Original Jerry Lee Lewis*
Crazy Arms/End of the Road/It'll Be Me/Whole Lotta Shakin' Goin' On/You Win Again/Great Balls of Fire/Down the Line/Breathless/High School Confidential/Fools Like Me/Breakup/I'll Make It All Up to You/Lovin' Up a Storm/Big Blon' Baby/Livin', Lovin' Wreck/What'd I Say
(1976)

CR 301 21: Nuggets Volume 1
*16 Rare Tracks by Jerry Lee Lewis*
Sweet Little Sixteen/Hello, Josephine/I've Been Twisting/It Won't Happen with Me/Ramblin' Rose/When I Get Paid/Love Made a Fool of Me/I Get the Blues When It Rains/In the Mood/Ubangi Stomp/It'll Be Me/Put Me Down/I'm Feeling Sorry/Ballad of Billy Joe/Baby, Baby, Bye Bye/Return of Jerry Lee
(1977)

CR 301 29: Nuggets Volume 2
*16 Rare Tracks By Jerry Lee Lewis*
Crazy Arms/Hillbilly Music/Turn Around/Night Train to Memphis/My Blue Heaven/It Hurt Me So/I Can't Help It/When the Saints Go Marching In/Whole Lot of Twistin' Goin' On/I'll Sail My Ship Alone/Friday Nights/Just Who Is to Blame/I Can't Trust Me in Your Arms Anymore/Hello, Hello, Baby/High-Powered Woman/Crawdad Hole
(1977)

CRM 2001: *The Essential Jerry Lee Lewis*—20 Original Rock 'n' Roll Hits
Whole Lotta Shakin'/Don't Be Cruel/Down the Line/Let the Good Times Roll/Jambalaya/High School Confidential/Jailhouse Rock/Lewis Boogie/Hound Dog/What'd I Say/Lovin' Up a Storm/Wild One/Great Balls of Fire/Singing the Blues/Little Queenie/Mean Woman Blues/Sixty-

1976: The years have been kind to him.

Minute Man/Lovesick Blues/Breath-less/It'll Be Me
(1978)

**FOREIGN SUN ALBUMS**
(Released in Europe on the Sun label)

6467 029: *Jerry Lee Lewis Rockin' and Free*
Pumpin' Piano Rock/Sixty-Minute Man/Ooby, Dooby/Mexicali Rose/Shame on You/When My Blue Moon Turns to Gold Again/Tomorrow Night/Ole Pal of Yesterday/All Night Long/Come What May/Please Release Me/Wild One/Hound Dog/Rock 'n' Roll Ruby/Born to Lose/Little Green Valley/Crazy Heart/Long Gone Lonesome Blues/My Carolina Sunshine Girl/Friday Night/Sick and Tired/So Long I'm Gone
(Many titles previously unissued)
(July, 1974)

NL 579: *Many Moods of Jerry Lee Lewis*
Big Blon' Baby/Matchbox/I'm Feeling Sorry/Livin', Lovin' Wreck/The Ballad of Billy Joe/Ubangi Stomp/Put Me Down/Hello, Hello, Baby/Baby, Baby, Bye Bye/It Won't Happen with Me/I know What It Means/Billy Boy
(1973)

6641 162: *Jerry Lee Lewis Rockin' Up a Storm*
Lewis Boogie/Great Balls of Fire/Whole Lotta Shakin' Goin' On/Breathless/Little Queenie/Let's Talk About Us/Lovin' Up a Storm/High School Confidential/Teenage Letter/What'd I Say/Good Golly Miss Molly/Mean Woman Blues/Breakup/Money (That's What I Want)/Johnny B. Goode/Hello, Josephine/Sweet Little Sixteen/Good Rockin' Tonight/C. C. Rider/Jailhouse Rock/Drinkin' Wine Spo-dee-o-dee/Jambalaya (On the Bayou)/As Long as I Live/Milkshake Mademoiselle/Pink Pedal Pushers/Save the Last Dance for Me/Carry On/In the Mood (The Hawk)

The piano on which young Jerry Lee learned to play. It now resides in his home at Coro Lake, Mississippi.

(Double album compiled in England)
(Apr. 1974)

NY 6: *Jerry Lee Lewis Collectors Edition*
I Don't Love Nobody/Milkshake Mademoiselle/Just Who Is to Blame/Rockin' the Boat of Love/Set My Mind at Ease/Ooby, Dooby/Carry On/My Quadroon/Rock 'n' Roll Ruby/Wild One/Slippin' Around/My Bonnie
(No Date Available)

SQ 20.067: *Jerry Lee Lewis Early Rock 'n' Roll*
Hand Me Down My Walking Cane/My Blue Heaven/Will the Circle Be Unbroken/If the World Keeps On Turning/Old Time Religion/You're the Only Star in My Blue Heaven/Crawdad Song/You Are My Sunshine/Waiting for a Train/Carry Me Back to Old Virginia/Silver Threads/Deep Elem Blues
(No Date Available)

HJS 168: *The Very Best of Jerry Lee Lewis*
Whole Lotta Shakin' Goin' On/Sweet Little Sixteen/High School Confidential/Jailhouse Rock/Good Golly Miss Molly/Hello, Josephine/Great Balls of Fire/Night Train to Memphis/Mean Woman Blues/Down the Line/C. C. Rider/Ramblin' Rose
(No Date Available)

**MOVIE SOUNDTRACK ALBUM**
SP 6500: *American Hot Wax*
(Original soundtrack album from the Paramount motion picture on the A & M Label)
Whole Lotta Shakin' Goin' On/Great Balls of Fire
(Recorded live, 1978)

**LOW BUDGET ALBUMS (DESIGN)**
Design 165: *Rocking with Jerry Lee Lewis*

Bonnie B./Lewis Boogie/I'll Make It All Up to You/It Hurt Me So (1963)

## LOW BUDGET ALBUMS (PICKWICK)

**JS-6120:** *Jerry Lee Lewis Rural Route #1*
Frankie and Johnny/Hillbilly Music/Lewis Boogie/C. C. Rider/Down the Line/Will the Circle Be Unbroken/It'll Be Me/Billy Boy/End of the Road (Jan. 1972)

**SPC-3344:** *Jerry Lee Lewis Drinkin' Wine Spo-dee-o-Dee*
Drinkin' Wine Spo-dee-o-dee/Just Because/Wedding Bells/It's a Hang-Up, Baby/Corinna, Corinna/Holdin' On/Dream Baby (How Long Must I Dream)/Memphis Beat/Big Boss Man (May 1973)

**SPC-3224:** *Jerry Lee Lewis High Heel Sneakers*
Hound Dog/Hallelujah I Love Her So/Sticks and Stones/Flip, Flop, and Fly/Baby, Hold Me Close/Crying Time/Got You on My Mind/You Went Back on Your Word/Too Young (July 1970)

## BUDGET ALBUMS (BUCKBOARD)

**BBS-1025:** *Jerry Lee Lewis The "Killer" Rocks On*
Great Balls of Fire/How's My Ex Treating You/What'd I Say/Johnny B. Goode/Save the Last Dance for Me/Sweet Little Sixteen/Little Queenie/Breathless/Mean Woman Blues (No Date Available)

## BUDGET ALBUMS (SUNNYVALE)

**9330-905:** *The Sun Story Volume 5 Jerry Lee Lewis*
Breathless/High School Confidential/Breakup/Frankie and Johnny/Hong Kong Blues/Hound Dog/Jailhouse Rock/Let the Good Times Roll/Let's Talk About Us/Lovesick Blues/Lovin' Up a Storm/Milkshake Mademoiselle (1977)

The last album for Mercury/Phonogram, after a fifteen-year association.

## BOOTLEG ALBUMS
(Rare Sound Records)

**1114:** *Rock and Roll with Jerry Lee*
Great Balls of Fire/Milkshake Mademoiselle/Never Be Ashamed of You/We Three/Mexicali Rose/Georgia on My Mind/My Baby/Tutti Fruitti/White Christmas/Don't Be Cruel/I Got a Woman/Great Balls of Fire/Shakin'/Jailhouse Rock/Interview BBC/High Heel Sneakers (No Date Available)

## BOOTLEG ALBUM (MULE RECORDS)

**201:** *Rockin' Jerry Lee Lewis*
Rockin' Jerry Lee/Danny Boy/Johnny B. Goode/I Can't Help It/Wild Side of Life/It'll Be Me/That Lucky Old Sun/Amazing Grace/My Baby Don't Love No One But Me/Mystery Train/I Get the Blues When It Rains/It's the Real Thing (Coca-Cola commercial)/High Heel Sneakers/White Christmas/When the Saints Go Marching In/Down the Line/What'd I Say/My Friend Jesus (No Date Available)

(Most of the above performances were taped from television appearances or from the radio.)

## ELEKTRA ALBUMS

**6E-184:** *Jerry Lee Lewis*
Don't Let Go/Rita May/Every Day I Have To Cry/I Like It Like That/Number One Lovin' Man/Rockin' My Life Away/Who Will the Next Fool Be/(You've Got) Personality/I Wish I Was Eighteen Again/Rocking Little Angel (Apr. 18, 1979)

**6E-254:** *Jerry Lee Lewis When Two Worlds Collide*
Rockin' Jerry Lee/Who Will Buy the Wine/Love Game/Alabama Jubilee/Good Time Charlie's Got the Blues/When Two Worlds Collide/Good News Travels Fast/I Only Want a Buddy Not a Sweetheart/Honky-Tonk Stuff/Toot, Toot, Tootsie (Goodbye) (Mar. 3, 1980)

His first album for Electra/Asylum, 1979. Recorded in four days.

ELEKTRA SINGLES

E-46030-A: Rockin' My Life Away/I Wish I Was Eighteen Again
(Mar. 1979)

E-46067-A: Who Will the Next Fool Be/Rita May
(June 1979)

E-46591-A: When Two Worlds Collide/Good News Travels Fast
(Jan. 22, 1980)

E-46642-A: Honky Tonk Stuff/Rockin' Jerry Lee
(May 12, 1980)

FUTURE ALBUM

Sun 1008: *The Million Dollar Quartet* featuring Elvis Presley, Johnny Cash, Jerry Lee Lewis, and Carl Perkins
Don't Forbid Me/Peace in the Valley/I Won't Have to Cross Jordan Alone/The Old Rugged Cross/Blueberry Hill/Island of Golden Dreams
(probably recorded early in January 1957)

# Conclusion

In 1981 Jerry Lee celebrates his 25th year in show business. Through it all, two factors have remained constant: His amazing talent and the undying devotion of his millions of fans throughout the world.

There is no doubt that Jerry has suffered from an indifferent and often downright biased press for years. However, public opinion seems finally to be swinging his way. The critical acclaim that eluded him for most of his career is finally becoming his. He is being recognized as the legend he is, and rewarded accordingly. It's about time.

What's Jerry Lee Lewis really like? He's a singin', shoutin', Bible-spoutin', rompin', stompin', jivin', jumpin', hell of a man! He's not a Xerox of anyone. He's an innovator, not an imitator. He's an original. He's a rock 'n' roll rebel. A man often torn between the rigid religious upbringing of his youth and his talent. When asked recently about retiring he said, "If I stop now, I'd probably die, so with the Good Lord willing, I'd like to keep going. I love music that much."

The only predictable thing about the Killer is his complete *unpredictability*. The story of Jerry Lee Lewis is just beginning.